PEOPLE AT WAR

1939–1945

Also edited by Michael Moynihan

People at War 1914–1918

PEOPLE AT WAR

1939-1945

Edited by

Michael Moynihan

DAVID & CHARLES

NEWTON ABBOT LONDON VANCOUVER

0 7153 6274 7

Set in 11 on 13pt Baskerville and printed in Great Britain by John Sherratt & Son Ltd for David & Charles (Holdings) Limited South Devon House Newton Abbot Devon

Published in Canada by Douglas David & Charles Limited 3645 McKechnie Drive West Vancouver BC

Contents

Acknowledgements

I am greatly indebted to the Imperial War Museum for access to recently acquired war diaries and journals, from which the first two chapters of this book have been selected. I would like particularly to thank Mr Roderick Suddaby, Head of the Department of Documents, and Dr Christopher Dowling, Keeper of the Department of Education and Publications, for their assistance and advice.

People at War would not have been possible to compile without the support and encouragement of the Editor of *The Sunday Times*, Mr Harold Evans, and thanks are also due to Mr Michael Randall, Senior Managing Editor, Mr Derrik Mercer, News Editor, and Mr George Darby, Editorial Manager.

Finally I would like again to thank all those readers of *The Sunday Times* who submitted journals, diaries, letters and personal anecdotes in answer to our request for war stories. Space could be found for only a very small proportion, but all the material received has been passed on to the Imperial War Museum.

M.M.

Foreword

The idea for this book (and its World War I companion volume) followed an article in *The Sunday Times* which quoted from some of the latest 'finds' of the Imperial War Museum and invited readers to send in their own war stories. The response was overwhelming, and it is from the best of the material received, and from the best of the Imperial War Museum's recent acquisitions, that *People at War* has been compiled.

This second volume has been a more difficult selection to make than that on World War I, which was largely waged throughout on the Western Front. The last war was far more diffused, mobile and mechanised, and there is nothing to compare with the prolonged drama and agony of trench warfare, to which most of the first volume is devoted. But within the limits of the material available (notably missing was anything relating to the Royal Air Force) I have tried to give as representative a picture as possible of ordinary people caught up in a war being waged on many fronts.

What has emerged most strongly from the reading of scores of diaries, journals, letters and recollections of specific incidents, has been the vastly more significant part played by the civilian in the last war. To the fighting man on the Western Front, Blighty meant a return to a world of comparative peace and plenty, where jingoism prevailed, propaganda whipped up hatred of the Hun and women thrust white feathers at young men still in civilian attire. Though contemporary records indicate an almost hysterical civilian reaction to the sporadic air raids by Zeppelins and Gothas, the Home Front bore very little resemblance to the battlefield it became in the last war, when the serviceman overseas often had more cause to be apprehensive about his loved ones back home than they about him.

In the last war 60,595 civilians were killed in air raids in the United Kingdom compared with 1,413 in World War I (the ratio of military deaths was 264,443 to nearly a million). And it seemed only right to devote three chapters of this book to civilian diaries. The feeling that impelled so many to record their daily experiences on the Home Front is summed up by one of them, a Somerset housewife: 'Perhaps I felt dimly that we were assisting, however remotely, in historic events.'

A recent upsurge of interest in the two world wars (reflected particularly in a spate of television series and the mass bookstall sales of illustrated war histories) may well suggest, on the part of older generations, a nostalgic backward look to a time when Britain was still indisputably Great. Millions can still recall those dark days of 1940 when this island stood alone against the might of Hitler's Third Reich, and the stirring of the blood as we listened on the radio to Churchill's bulldog growl: 'We shall fight on the beaches, we shall fight on the landing grounds, we shall fight in the fields and in the streets, we shall fight in the hills. We shall never surrender.'

To millions more the last war is a tale told by the middle-aged and elderly, a mere chapter in history. Their conception of it is most likely coloured by films and television series—*The Longest Day, The Cruel Sea, Dam Busters, Bridge on the River Kwai, Colditz, Manhunt, Dad's Army.* They may see it as a sequence of real-life adventure stories. Or they may shrug it off in the dismissive terms used by a young newspaper critic who referred to the television series, 'Family at War', as being 'as grey and boring as the war itself'.

The war was, of course, both exciting and boring, drab and ennobling, challenging and repressive, tragic and fun (even walking in the black-out could be an adventure). And in these pages will be found an authentic flavour of what it was like to be living in times when one never quite knew what was going to happen next, when the individual's preoccupation with 'getting on' had to a large extent become subservient to a communal struggle and when one took for granted hazards and hardships that would have been unthinkable in peacetime.

The nation that heard Neville Chamberlain's sombre announcement on the radio, that bright Sunday morning of 3 September 1939, that Britain was again at war with Germany, was in a very different mood from the euphoric jubilation of 4 August 1914. For many there was a sense of relief that the period of appeasement was over and that an evil and ruthless dictatorship was to be challenged at last. Though the full measure of Hitler's crimes against humanity was yet to be revealed there was doubt in few minds that this was a just and inevitable war. There were few doubts either that it was to be total war, with the civilian no less at risk than the serviceman.

When the black-out clamped down that first night, the nation was keyed up to unimaginable horrors. Already over a million women and children had been evacuated to the countryside. On nightmare calculations by the Air Ministry that 600,000 dead and 1,200,000 injured might be expected in the first sixty days of war, some 200,000 hospital beds had been set aside for the first casualties, while stockpiles of collapsible coffins, made of cardboard or papiermâché, awaited the dead.

No one knew quite what to expect—something perhaps like those terrible scenes of London's destruction in the recently distributed film version of H. G. Wells's *The Shape of Things to Come*. I recall that when the first air raid sirens wailed over Merseyside my family sat in the basement kitchen, wearing their gas masks and biting on india rubbers as a precaution against perforation of the ear drums, while a solitary RAF plane, off course, passed high overhead in a radiant sunset.

The anti-climax of the eight months that followed, when almost nothing at all happened, became known as the Phoney War or Great Bore War. It ended on 10 May 1940 (the day Churchill took over the premiership from Chamberlain) with news that German tanks were thrusting into the Low Countries. With vague memories of 1914, the public now looked to the British and French armies to halt the enemy along another Western Front, if not to drive them back.

'We chalked "Berlin or Bust" on the sides of the waggons and joined the crazy rush of the BEF to a Belgium already doomed,' writes Private W. B. A. Gaze. No one had foreseen the German blitzkrieg (lightning war). Ten chaotic days later, along roads choked with pain-stricken refugees, Gaze was on the beaches of Dunkirk, witnessing the start of the 'miraculous' evacuation that saved 380,000 troops to fight again another day.

Britain's 'finest hour' had struck. 'We shall defend our island whatever the cost may be' was a Churchillian challenge that welded the nation together as never before. Only from hindsight does a faint air of the ridiculous underlie those three months of the invasion scare when we attuned ourselves to a homeland where pill-boxes, tank traps, road blocks bristled on all sides, where railway stations became anonymous and signposts pointed to nowhere, where 'walls had ears' and any stranger might be a fifth columnist or saboteur, where it became an offence to do a host of things from ringing church bells to failing to immobilise a parked car, and where over one-and-a-half million hastily trained men between the ages of 17 and 65 patrolled town and countryside in guerrilla bands, trigger-happy.

Dad's Army, television's most popular fictionalised series on the last war, is a prime example of how history can be reconstructed with seeming authenticity, but with a vital element missing. The characters and the settings ring true, but it is all a jolly charade. As a member of the Home Guard at the time, I vividly recall a telephone call at home in the early hours with urgent orders to report for duty. German parachutists were believed to have landed. With rifles at the ready, some of us stood guard until dawn in a rubbish dump on the outskirts of the town overlooking an insignificant branch railway line, while others, with dimmed torches, searched tunnels and track. Only the fact that the sky was completely overcast and it rained most of the time suggested to some that it might all be a false alarm.

Bombs, not parachutists, were to be Britain's lot. A total of 70,995 tons of high explosive, and innumerable incendiary bombs, were dropped during the war, destroying 220,000 homes and damaging nearly five million more. Predictably the blitz was easily the predominating subject matter of World War II records sent in by *Sunday Times* readers. And the two diaries selected (both set in London, where nearly half the total civilian deaths occurred) indicate how different could be the individual reaction.

Mrs Joan Veazey, who married a young curate in the Elephant and Castle district near the start of the 1940 blitz, which raged for seventy-six consecutive nights, writes with a tense gritting of the teeth about the nightmare that enveloped her. Describing her return from a briefly snatched honeymoon in the remote tranquillity of North Wales, she hints at the fear so many kept just under control. 'I watched the hills as the train passed. They looked darker and more lonely than when we came. The train seemed to go so quickly, and I felt my tummy turning over as I realised that soon we should hear that awful wailing siren again . . . '

Lionel King was eight when he kept a diary of the flying bomb assault on London in 1944, and he echoes the feeling of heightened awareness, of almost exhilarating excitement, that not only children could experience as the familiar world was transformed around one. In Mrs Veazey's description of her husband's church going up in flames many will recapture that breath-taking clutch of awe:

> The Altar caught alight and seemed to fold up and die before our eyes. The church burnt with white hot flames . . . The windows had gone, the wind changed its direction and fanned the flames to even greater heights. We could hear the

cries of the pigeons in the tower . . . The great bells fell from the top of the tower with a mighty rush of sparks and flames . . .

For over four years air raids swept sporadically over Britain in a series of great waves. The blitz was the perennial talking-point and to some extent detracted from the exploits of our far-flung fighting men. World War II, indeed, presented a confusing picture of several wars going on at once—in the Far East, Russia, North Africa, Europe, in the air and at sea. And in very few of the British army campaigns was there anything approaching the personal contact with the enemy that rivets attention in World War I accounts of trench warfare.

Among battle descriptions provided by ex-servicemen, even two diaries by men who fought from the beaches at Anzio and Normandy have an impersonal air about them and lack cohesive tension. Ironically the experiences of prisoners-of-war can seem more dramatic and eventful, like those of Private Norman Norris, captured in Crete, who spent four years as a 'slave labourer' in a Berlin stalag, on the receiving end of the Allies' massed air raids, finally liberated by the Russians. Thousands of Other Rank POWs like him must have winced at the 'officers and gentlemen' depiction of prison life in the widely acclaimed television series, *Colditz*.

But for many servicemen and women the last war was a comparatively cushy and uneventful interlude to Civvy Street, personal responsibilities abnegated and replaced by a resigned fatalism. The daily routine at a home base might be boring, but servicemen fed better than civilians and there were outlets enough for high spirits, as indicated in army cook Ted Smith's ebullient account of the goings-on in barracks and camps. Even his description of a brief spell of active service in Algiers and Tunisia has an hilarious savour to it. 'What a life, what a laugh,' he nostalgically sums up.

For much of the war Britain was a base for overseas as well as British servicemen. In its early stages one could trace the progress of the German blitzkrieg by the nationalities of 'freedom fighters' appearing in the streets—Czechs, Poles, French, Dutch, Norwegians, Belgians. Their uniforms, like those of Dominion and Colonial troops, became part of the cosmopolitan daily scene. Then came the Yanks.

Far more than the World War I doughboy, who made his appearance only in the last year of the war, the GI became an accepted part of life on the Home Front. To austerity Britain they were seen as prodigally affluent cousins from a land flowing with milk and honey. And to the British serviceman, with only a quarter of their basic pay and with nothing approaching the largesse of their camps, they were often objects of envy, even hostility, particularly as holding an unfair advantage in the pursuit of 'a bit of skirt'. But, armed with a perceptive 'Short Guide to Great Britain', which delineated the character of the typical native and warned against brashness and exhibitionism, they made far more friends than enemies among civilians up and down the country, and their very presence seemed to bring victory that much nearer.

Up to D-Day nearly a million and a half servicemen from overseas had been billeted in Britain. And for many the abiding memories of the war are less of its darker side than of the comradeship that flourished with a common cause at stake. Just as social barriers dissolved when Britain lay open to invasion or when the bombs rained down, so barriers of language and nationality were set aside as the Allies geared themselves to the final assault on Hitler's Europe.

In a recent tour in the United States I met Americans in many walks of life who spontaneously responded to an English accent with effusive memories of the war days here. England to them still means, not a downgraded world power, but a sleepy village near an army camp, a home that had made them one of the family, conviviality in a friendly pub. War, it is often said, can bring out the best as well as the worst in people, and there are intangible effects of the last war that still happily linger.

There is something symbolic in a footnote to the wartime diary kept by Mrs Lee-Michell, near whose home in Somerset thousands of Americans were stationed. For a short spell early in 1944 a young Texan called Bill was billeted on them. He was ordered to report to camp shortly before D-Day, and she never heard of him again. But she still has in her possession the battle-jacket he left behind. A grandmother now, she wears it for gardening.

Far away and long ago seem those wartime years. But they come alive again in these pages, and they are worth recalling. As on that morning of 6 June 1944, when Texan Bill and so many others like him had crossed from fortress Britain into battle, and a Somerset housewife jotted another entry in her Charles Letts' Popular Diary: 'Mike called me in from a pre-breakfast prowl in the dewy garden: "I think the Second Front has started." We thought it might, as last night the planes flew off as usual but did not return . . . Sick with excitement all day, hoping and praying . . . '

Michael Moynihan

1 Dunkirk Driver

'Soldiers are not fortune-tellers, so we chalked "Berlin or Bust" on the sides of the waggons and joined the crazy rush of the BEF to a Belgium already doomed.' So Private W. B. A. Gaze, 7618147, Royal Army Ordnance Corps, recalled the sunny morning of 20 May 1940, when his Field Workshop set off for a 'destination unknown' along the road to Brussels. 'Perhaps we were best in our happy delusion. No amount of foreknowledge would have avoided the tragedy into which we were so lightheartedly rushing.'

Gaze was writing of his experiences on his return to England eight months later, after being one of the first British prisoners-of-war to escape from a German Stalag across occupied France and Spain to Gibraltar. They were in some ways unique. After the retreat of the British Expeditionary Force before the German Panzers and Stukas, Gaze was among the first on the Dunkirk beaches. But he was not among the 225,000 British troops who escaped back to England in that 'miraculous' evacuation. Through a series of misadventures he found himself attached to a military hospital, driving ambulances loaded with wounded to and from the docks through constant shellfire and bombing. He was still driving after the Germans entered the shattered port. 'Dunkirk Driver' is his title for the 60,000-word journal, partly based on a diary he kept at the time, from which these extracts are taken.

Gaze's war record is unusual in other ways. He was 37, married with three children, when he enlisted in December 1939 after a radio appeal had been made for Army drivers. He had earlier applied for a commission on the strength of the Certificate A he had gained as a schoolboy in 1920 after four years' OTC training, but got tired of waiting. He was an auctioneer and valuer by profession, but also ran a 200-acre farm near Diss in Norfolk as a side-line. This he omitted to mention for fear it would be regarded as a reserved occupation. A hankering for adventure as well as a sense of duty spurred him. Both were to be satisfied.

It was on 11 April 1940 that Gaze's Field Workshop of sixty-five vehicles landed in a vast convoy at Cherbourg. He was astonished to find no evidence of air raid precautions in France, lights blazing at night, no gas masks carried, 'everyone light-hearted and confident, only the absence of men a reminder of war'. And for much of the month that preceded the launching of the German offensive into Holland, Belgium and Luxemburg, there was something of the atmosphere of 'a glorified picnic' as the convoys moved from camp to camp. They moved over the battlefields of World War I through towns and villages 'totally rebuilt and even in parts getting shabby again'. By 19 May Gaze had reached the village of Vieux Berquin near the Belgian frontier, a village obliterated in World War I.

Next day, 'Berlin or Bust' on their waggons, real war began for Gaze.

'Through Louvain and Renaix, the population cheering every waggon, handing us beer, chocolates, cigarettes and anything else we asked for. On one side of the road an unending stream of British Infantry in trucks, Bren gun carriers, guns, service corps, ordnance, each convoy with its quota of Austin 8's and dispatch riders, on the other side a still thicker stream, the significance of which we did not yet realise, the first of the refugees.

'These were the refugees who had not yet experienced much danger or hardship, not too uncomfortably packed in cars and lorries, with their bedding and plenty of fuel and provisions. They were happy to see the British Army come to relieve their country. They thought their pilgrimage would soon be over. "Bon voyage!" they called. "Bon voyage à vous"—"bientôt revenir", we replied and went singing on our way.

'At Renaix we began to see a few refugees in waggons and on cycles, and even on foot, also a few scattered units of the Belgian Army going in a direction we did not expect. We took the main Brussels road to a village about 30 km. south of Brussels. Here, by the railway crossing, several houses were bombed, and we heard the tragic story of a troop train machine gunned from the air. The driver was not hurt and drew up his train at the station here. Blood was running out of all the carriages, and the story was that every man was killed.

'Now the road was literally flooded with refugees. There were still plenty of cars, but now the old crocks began to go past, vehicles that evidently had not lately been on the road staggered by under immense freights of people and their possessions. The number of people crowded into lorries was amazing. They were not so cheerful now, the bombardment of Brussels was commencing. There were also plenty of people on cycles, but the larger part of the procession, and by far the most tragic, was composed of the peasants from the Louvain district, and the poor people of Brussels on foot.

'The peasants had already come a fair distance. There was a proportion of the larger farmers who could put a team of four good Belgian chestnut horses on to one of the immensely long and large waggons of the country. These great vehicles comfortably held one or more families with all their household goods and plenty of provisions, fodder etc. In some cases a tilt was rigged up, covered waggon style. On the waggon would be room for one or two calves or pigs. Occasionally the master of a large farm would have quite a cavalcade, two or three waggon teams with his sons or workmen and their families, colts and foals and cows tied behind, and in the rear the farmer and his wife in a smart market cart or car. These refugees were well dressed, and cheerfully made the best of things. Only the old men and women, some of whom had fled before the Germans already in 1914, and even in 1870, showed by their looks the reality of the tragedy.

'But most of the peasants were not of this comfortable class. An old horse, or perhaps a pair, towing the three-wheeled tumbril of Belgium, generally with another in tow, and a handcart on a string behind, transported all their poor goods. Sometimes they had loaded some incongruous implement on the cart, perhaps the only machine of any value on the farm. A few had a cow or a colt behind the tumbril, or a sow in a wheeled crate tied on behind. The old grandfather or grannie rode in the tumbril, minding the babies, but the fathers, mothers, sons and daughters had to walk and help the poor old horse.

'The foot passengers were in multitudes. Poor families from Brussels transported their children, their beds and a few bits of furniture on a big hand cart, if they were very lucky with a dog in the shafts, but more usually the woman in the shafts, the man pushing behind, the bigger children helping with cords, and, as often as not, an old woman on top of the load. Others had their bicycles, not to ride upon but to support ungainly bundles of bedding and one or two children. And the prams—usually the party consisted of an elderly woman pushing the pram with a baby hidden under bedding and other packages, her daughter carrying a bigger child, and other children, according to size, either dangling miserably tired at their mother's heels or helping the grannie with the pram by means of a string.

'Other people, better dressed, were obviously quite unused to walking 3 kilometres, much less 80, but marched bravely on, refusing to give in to the evident misery of their feet. Also there were many groups of men from twenty to forty-five years of age, few carrying coats and mostly wearing light canvas shoes, but all carrying a blanket. These were the Belgian troops, not yet called up, answering the summons to a depot, always, I noticed, comfortably in the rear. And already there was the occasional small party of Belgian soldiers going the same way as the refugees.

'Next day the crowds of refugees were as thick as ever on the road, and contained many surprises. There were many bare chassis from motor show rooms, with a few boards tacked across the frames on which an altogether improbable number of people crowded. The policemen of Brussels evacuated on their cycles, and even, to our greater surprise, the firemen on their fire engines. A stream of Belgian troops of all arms was nearly continuous, and they were not under much discipline, and occasionally we saw French troops also going south. The flow of British troops to the front was not now quite so continuous, and on our return we met a battalion of infantry, which we had seen the previous day advancing, marching back, rather footsore and very puzzled about their orders.'

For the next two days the Recovery Section to which Gaze was attached carried on with its primary task of keeping roads used by troops clear of crashed and broken-down vehicles. But when they, too, joined the chaotic retreat—hearing all the time the sound of distant gunfire, seeing the night sky lit by pillars of fire from blazing towns, on occasion diving for shelter from swooping Messerschmitts and Stukas—he felt frustrated at having no real function to perform. 'We should have burnt the waggons and gone to the help of the infantry.'

Then on the afternoon of 26 May, with British and French troops fighting a desperate rearguard action as the bulk of the army headed for Dunkirk, he found himself engaged in what he describes as one of his eeriest experiences—the rescue of a marooned body of men in what had briefly become a No Man's Land in the World War I-haunted neighbourhood of Ypres.

'About 4 o'clock we received an urgent order to unload all the stores out of the three-ton waggons and volunteers were called for for a convoy. Drivers who were married were told not to volunteer. The SQMS frowned on my request to take the French Ford van I had found abandoned and taken over two days before, but the Adjutant let me go. We set off in a convoy of three motor buses, six three-ton Austins, my little van, a Lieutenant and a staff sergeant with a light car, and motor cyclists.

'The road was lined for miles with French and British infantry, all pointed towards Bergues, and waiting for the troops which were fighting the last covering action a mile or two away on each side. Every mile or two was a barricade of old farm waggons, etc, generally defended by a field gun or a tank, and guarded by grim, determined French infantrymen.

'We drove through a dark, moonless night. It was very quiet—in fact we had retreated rather faster than Jerry could come up. We got mixed up with a big ambulance convoy, but extricated ourselves. With the dawn we arrived in the village which was our destination, and found the men we had been sent for. About 300 men had apparently been discharged from hospital or returned from leave into this village, which was a centre of distribution. When the retreat started they were left without transport, mostly without rifles, many with neither gas mask or tin hat.

'We loaded up half the men and made our way back. I had a dozen in the little Ford. One of the motor buses conked out, but our orders were no delay and no repairs, so we shared out the passengers and carried on. The great convoy we had seen upon the road waiting for the troops had mainly gone. Only the Frenchmen at the barriers remained. We dropped our passengers close to Bergues, and turned round for the second trip.

'This second trip was a curious experience. All the troops were gone. We met an occasional lorry bringing back the Frenchmen from the barricades, but that was all. We hardly realised what this implied at the time. Personally I felt rather as if I was navigating a boat through the tide race at Yarmouth at dead low water. I suppose that is a fairly apt simile and explains why we got to the village again, and got the other 150 away, just at the turn of the tide.

'The second motor bus had gone into a ditch on the way out and been abandoned and we had some other breakdowns, so all our remaining vehicles were well loaded. In my little Ford they had to sit down the middle to trim the ship! As usual the weather was wonderful, but over this sun-drenched countryside brooded an uncanny silence. There was no one about.

'Then, as we drew near Bergues, the silence was broken. The miserable Belgians were marching home, if you could call it marching, moving in their usual unsoldierly manner, one man pushing two or three men's rifles on a bicycle and the others walking behind, some on horses or driving waggons, an occasional motor vehicle. They were walking back home to give themselves up. No doubt they hoped Hitler would have a special welcome for the traitors who had let us down. He had, as I later learned. Say what you like about the German, he is a soldier, and had no hesitation in showing these "troops" how much he appreciated their action.'

After a hurried mid-day meal, all the convoy vehicles were destroyed except for Gaze's van, on to which all the men's kit was loaded and in which he drove with the staff sergeant and two others, whilst the rest marched the ten kilometres to Dunkirk. The road was full of hurrying troops. Already the city was ablaze at many points.

'The Colonel and the Adjutant, with the main body, which had arrived without any losses, had found comfortable temporary quarters in good sized houses in a street in the centre of the town. But we had not been there many minutes when the bombs began to fall, a salvo every few minutes, and most of them close. It was, in fact, this afternoon the dive bombers literally battered the centre of the town to pieces.

'Soon houses were on fire in our street, and the explosions were shaking our house, though strangely enough a little garden courtyard, with a glazed verandah at the side, remained, for the moment, a quiet haven, even the glass unbroken. Foraging about the house, it was peculiar to walk through the undisturbed rooms with good, expensive furniture, to examine the photographs of the —no doubt—highly respected master and mistress of the house, and to think that all this would inevitably be, before long, ashes and rubble. The beds were very tempting, but somehow seemed too close to the roof. Anyhow, the gentleman had a good wine cellar! The bombing became incessant, and we were soon distributed in the cellars of half a dozen houses.

'We were quite cheerful on the whole because we heard the navy was sending fourteen ships at dusk. We imagined the big guns driving off the bombers, and a nice, easy trip to England. During the afternoon I went to reconnoitre. Towards the waterfront the devastation was most apparent. The Town Hall was in flames, and here I saw the most heroic action. Two or three elderly firemen continued, undisturbed by the bombs, to play their useless jets upon the flames. The futility of their action! Their town obviously doomed, no doubt their own houses flaming, dead men lying round their engine, bomb splinters holing their hoses—but these old fellows could not let the "Hotel de Ville" burn down unhindered while they lived.

'It was a touchy business crossing the square, with too many silent reminders of what happened if one was not under cover when the Stukas dived. One poor fellow will always remain fixed in my mind. A freak of the explosion had not only taken his trousers, but his private parts, mercifully his life as well.

'The harbour basin was full of fishing craft and little boats, and no one had yet realised their possibilities. A few odd men were about on the quays on the same errand as myself. But there was no boat and no news of any boat. I returned to the cellars. About four o'clock a rumour ran round that the boats would soon be here, and all should go on the sand dunes. By their edge was the French barracks, evacuated. I put the little van, loaded with the kit, in the yard and waited in the barracks because, though very smelly, they were much healthier than the sand dunes. We waited about till perhaps six o'clock and then set off for the beach, the van trailing behind it yards of the tramway wires which hung down all over the place. Our officers made some sort of a muster, and everyone seemed to be present.

'The nightmare of this night on Dunkirk Beach has been many

times described. I will not attempt to emulate anyone else's catalogue of horrors, but merely describe the events of the night as I saw them. We collected round the houses and shops which lined the one-time pleasure beach. I drove the little van into a space where there had been a shop and left it there. Very few came to collect their kit after all our trouble. Our officers divided us up into 50s. There were great numbers of men on the sea front not organised in any way, and the 50 to which I was allotted gradually grew till it was 100. Some brass hat turned up and split it into two 50s, and so I was separated from the Unit.

'The 50s proceeded on to the wide sandy beach and lay down in circles, at intervals, to see what was coming next. Jerry had slackened his efforts for an hour or two, presumably while he had his supper, but now returned, and the rain of bombs began again on the town. The houses on the sea front behind us were very soon a mass of roaring flames, the dock buildings on our left were being attacked with heavier stuff, and the beach and sea were flooded with crimson light, as bright as the most powerful artificial light. At an altitude of about 300 feet was a sort of roof, solid black smoke which reflected the flames, and which, under Providence, was undoubtedly our salvation, for there were 20,000 men on the beach at the absolute mercy of the Stukas.

'After a bit a British destroyer appeared in the distance. The next arrival was a string of three Thames barges, one with a motor, which was moored about 400 yards from the shore, for a purpose I have never fathomed—they were still there, one at least undamaged, a week later. Now the Stukas turned their attention to the beach, dropping first a line of flares on their left. We thought we were for it when we heard the bombs swishing down. There was nothing at all to be done, except to sit tight, or at best try to dig a little hole with a rifle. The fourteen ships, of which we had heard so much, now appeared—drifters, each towing two boats. The first boats motored slowly to the beach, and the great evacuation had begun.

'It was painfully slow work as each boat should only take 50 men (as a matter of fact, in the beautiful calm weather, they took a lot more), and there were rows and rows of little groups lower down the beach. We had been unfortunate in being redivided while others were gaining a good position, and still more unfortunate in our officer. I don't know who this gentleman was, but he was a man sadly lacking in initiative. While he kept us in our one spot, the other 50s were all slowly moving towards the sea. From first to last we hardly moved at all.

'We stuck like this for five hours altogether. Every ten minutes or so the bombers came over, always from west to east, and we crouched in the little pits we had dug as the bombs came whistling down. At the west end of the beach, near the quays, many of them found a mark, but where we were lying very few were hit, and nearly all the bombs fell into the sea. Occasionally a line of flares came down close, but the pall of smoke from the blazing town saved us. And so the boats went painfully slowly backwards and forwards to the drifters, half an hour or more to a trip.

'Meanwhile, on the sea front and the top of the beach, were constant fresh arrivals. These began to creep down the beach and insinuate themselves into the 50s, so that the groups became less defined. Suddenly there was a rush from the top of the beach, and our disciplined wait of five hours was in vain. As the men rushed down the beach, a naval officer ran forward and shouted that all could not get on the boats, but he now had a ship at the quay and advised us to try that.

'I jettisoned my kit and was one of the first in the rush towards the pier to the west of the beach, which was here pitted with bomb craters and littered with dead men. Two men, staggering along with a wounded man on a stretcher, called me to help them. This, of course, let all the others go past. We eventually got the wounded man to the narrow quay. It was by now crowded with men, trying to shelter under a low, concrete wall as they moved, inch by inch, towards the ship at the far end. It seemed a hopeless endeavour, particularly as dawn was at hand, and the chatter of machine guns could now and again be heard from the planes. I went back to the beach again to see about a boat.

'Queues were now waiting in the water. I joined one of them, but only went in up to my knees, for I could see men up to their necks and swimming, fighting for the boats, and naval officers using their revolvers. Seeing how hopeless it was to get a boat and not wishing to join in a fight with my own mates, also having lost sight of my own Unit entirely, I considered that I was at liberty to try to do something for myself, and it appeared there might be a chance of living a while longer by getting off the beach.

'I met with a man in our recovery section and we set off to find the little boats I had seen earlier. But we could not locate the harbour basin and continued along the canal until we found ourselves on the outskirts of the town, in the direction of Calais. A French lorry was moving out and we climbed aboard. After about eight kilometres the lorry turned off into the country and we left it, it being our intention to work along the coast.

'A convoy of British ambulances came up. They had orders for Dunkirk, but had turned back as it seemed too hopeless. The Corporal in charge agreed with my idea to go to a fishing village in search of a boat and row over. Near the beach we met a French coastguard, but could not argue him into letting us have a boat, and the Corporal decided to drive back to Dunkirk again. The area behind the docks was now being fiercely bombarded and we came to a standstill. The driver I was riding with, whose ambulance was empty, said he was going back. The Corporal said he was going to try to get through, so we parted, my friend staying with the Corporal. My driver followed the Calais Canal a few kilometres, then crossed it, and eventually came to the end of a sandy road near the sea, not far from the blazing oil refinery which had covered Dunkirk with smoke for days.

'We got out and walked, and after a bit arrived at the blown-up bridge over the moat of Fort L'Ouest. We were admitted, and found a place to lie under a blanket for an hour or two with the members of a Red Cross train who had sheltered at the Fort when their train became too hot to live in. The Red Cross train party and the ambulance driver went off, during a lull, to Dunkirk to embark, but their officer refused me as I was nothing to do with the Red Cross.

'I was temporarily attached to the French Marines at the Fort, and received a long French rifle and bayonet, after which I spent the day carrying shells over the planks where the bridges had been blown up. Two of their coast defence guns were trained on Bergues, where the Germans were now reported to be, and every half hour or so they fired them off, with an immense amount of enthusiasm, blowing the "Alerte" on the bugles and unnecessarily running about. They were very cheerful and hospitable, had plenty to eat and unlimited "pinard" [wine].

'No one had much idea where the Germans were, but the Commandant would not let me out of the Fort until he had some definite idea of the whereabouts of some other British unit to send me to. After so many nights with little or no rest I was miserably tired, and after their last meal (La Soupe) I got hold of a big French blanket and got down in the straw to a magnificent night's rest of twelve or thirteen hours.

'Next morning, wanting something to do as I was still not permitted to go to look for other British troops, I went to the armoury. The Marines had been venturing down to the town between bombardments, and had found, not only one or two British lorries, but quite a lot of miscellaneous weapons and ammunition, which they did not understand. I cleaned up an anti-tank gun for them, filled up the magazines with ammunition, and arranged to take this over in the event of attack. Then I found a serviceable, but very sandy, Lewis gun. This I took to pieces and cleaned and got it going again. They had plenty of British ammunition, but no Lewis gun magazines. So I persuaded them to let me go with the next party to Dunkirk to look for them. And that is how I left Fort L'Ouest.

'Riding in a British lorry they had found in the streets, we passed the burning refinery, which threw a great heat across the road, and made for Dunkirk. There was a temporary lull in the bombardment, and quite a lot of people in the streets, civilians who had come out of the ruins, and French and British troops, the former rather aimless, hunting for loot more than anything, the latter moving always towards the docks. A woman rushed out of a demolished shop, shouting for help, so we stopped.

'A lorry, which had evidently been machine gunned stood outside, and inside were seven badly wounded men. Apparently after the machine gunning their mates had put them in the shop to await assistance, and gone on. One man was obviously a goner, his internal organs were laid bare, so we did not disturb his last hour with further pain, but left him in charge of the poor woman, and put the others in the lorry.

'The front tyres were burst and the radiator holed, as well as the whole vehicle being shot full of bullet holes, but fortunately the engine started, and eventually I managed to drive it to the British Military Hospital (the 11th Casualty Clearing Station) at the Chateau Rosendale on the outskirts of the town, the engine very hot but not actually refusing until we got to the door. Orderlies came out and got the men on to stretchers and took them in. A very worried-looking RAMC Sergeant Major came out and told me to put the lorry somewhere out of the way if it would go no further. Then he asked me if I would mind doing a trip or two to the docks as four drivers had deserted. As I had driven our town volunteer ambulance for a dozen or more years I could not very well refuse, and proceeded to find up an ambulance.'

From 29 May to 5 June, when the Germans entered Dunkirk, Gaze was occupied day and night in driving load after load of wounded men from the hospital to the quayside and the ships to England. The ambulance convoys were soon running the gauntlet of shells from German howitzers at Bergues as well as bombs.

'The days and nights ran into one another with never a night's rest. One has difficulty in fitting together afterwards the jigsaw remembrance of a nightmare.

'The streets began to get very full of bomb holes, though working parties pulled bricks from the shattered houses into them and generally tried to keep the roads passable. The town began to carry a beastly smell of burnt meat. I doubt there were some horrid sights when the Germans looked through the ruins later.

'I found a passably safe method of getting from Chateau Rosendale to the quays, based on Jerry's undoubted endeavour to spare the Red Cross. By waiting till after a salvo, one could dash along the canal road and gain the Civil Hospital, wait for the next lot and make another dash through about half a mile of streets and a wide open space to the shelter of the line of Bastions at the docks.'

Gaze, who had been picked to lead the ambulance convoys, recounts many grim happenings on trips through the town and while helping with the wounded on the quayside, often under bomb attack. On 31 May the hospital was, officially, cleared.

'Had there been any realisation of the position we should have shut the doors and fixed up a dressing station on the quay. This would have saved the ultimate capture of more than two hundred wounded men, but unfortunately our officers, in the absence of further orders, left the door open. The battle was closer now and, within another hour or two, we had a full house again, a garden full of ambulances and no one to take them away.

'That evening another driver and myself were sent to the Bastion, but there the wounded men from the beach were dressed and sent *back* through the streets to our doomed hospital. After one or two journeys I realised I was only carrying men to captivity or death, so forgot my orders and refused to take any more away from the quays. Whatever boat they were put on, and in whatever state, it was better than Rosendale.'

Next evening Gaze led the last convoy from the hospital to the quay.

'Through the interminable night we waited for the boats. Another driver and myself made a bed of blankets under my ambulance and slept as well as we could, but the bombs kept crashing down, and the French fortress guns were duelling with Bergues. When the time came to move at last, half the ambulances had no drivers. They had caught the boats. I had to take four to the end of the quay, where I was engaged for quite a while in clearing away a litter of trucks, cars and ambulances left behind in the evacuation. A horse was wandering miserably about. Another was dead. He went in the canal. The waggons went on the beach, those that would go pushing those that wouldn't. Vehicles worth thousands of pounds were pushed over down the sides of the canal, and at last the quay end was cleared for use.

'About 200 German prisoners were put on the boats that day. They were fairly fresh and cheerful. No doubt we were pleased to take them, but they took up 200 places for our men in the boats. While I was at the docks news came through that there would be no more hospital ships. 25 men and 4 officers were to stay at the hospital with about 350 wounded. The remaining drivers were ordered home. Lots were drawn. But I never heard of these orders, and when I got back to Rosendale I was the last driver in Dunkirk.'

Next day the French tent hospital in the grounds of Chateau Rosendale was bombed, and Gaze was kept busy driving French wounded to an improvised hospital in a brewery. The British officers were still trying to pretend to their patients that they would all get away, and on 3 June they decided to try and get the walking wounded away on any available destroyer.

'Two of the officers volunteered to drive lorries, and we advised all the wounded who thought they could walk, scramble or crawl along with help, to get in. About 100 were loaded up, and it is a great pity the orders were not made more definite, because many more could have gone the same way.

'This time we had to do a lot of carrying ourselves on the quays. I was stretcher bearing for an hour or two with one of our officers and sometimes with a sailor, up the narrow, wooden stage which leads up to the quay end. The German guns at Bergues had our range and shells were bursting about twenty feet up all round the stage. There was not one with our names on it, and we got all the men aboard. I wanted to have another load, but the officers were certain it would be too late as this was to be the last boat, so we left the old naval officer sitting in his chair at the quay end (thousands must remember his dogged, inspiring presence) and also left an ambulance which one of our officers had nearly turned over, balanced on two wheels and a heap of timber. I had the chance to go home by this last boat, but with twenty-five ambulances full of helpless, wounded men back at the hospital, and not another driver, it was a chance obviously impossible to take advantage of. So we returned to Rosendale and the evacuation was over.'

Early next morning, 4 June, Gaze made one last, unavailing trip to the docks with seven wounded men.

'No more boats. A French destroyer at the extreme end of the pier, and, far away at St-Malo-Les-Bains, another, ready to move off. It was quiet now. The ruined buildings sent up only a little smoke, and in the beautiful clear morning could be seen the sunken ships all round the inner harbour, and out to sea as well, a Thames barge still floating at anchor untouched, the quays, canal sides and beaches crowded with abandoned waggons, many dead upon the beach, and the greater desolation because it was so obviously the end.

'The Navy had gone. The AA guns were gone. The wireless van was scuttled. We could hope for nothing more. A few Frenchmen were going off to their distant boats, but for us it was finished. A French tug lay near at hand, but they refused my patients, and, very sad, I had to take them back. On the road home we passed a horrible sight. Two bombs of very large calibre had burst in masses of men. One circle was Frenchmen. On the outside, bodies, in the unnatural atttudes always seen in men blasted out of life in an instant by direct hits, nearer the middle incomplete parts, a medley of heads and trunks and arms, in the middle—nothing, a dozen poor fellows gone up literally as mincemeat. The other group—identical—were Englishmen.'

Back at Chateau Rosendale, elegant residence of a wealthy Dunkirker, with formal gardens and two acres of ground, they awaited the Germans.

'The battle was getting closer. The French horse artillery and tanks were moving towards Zudcoote, four kilometres to the east, doing what they could. The shells were bursting among the houses just over the wall. During the night someone had altered the red cross on the tower and put it towards Bergues, but it was not hanging down properly, so I went up and fixed it with weights in the bottom corner.

'The shells were passing about thirty yards away as I stood on the tower. They were time fuse shells, bursting at the end of their travel, and I thought that Jerry was aiming to a nicety to save the hospital. In fact I was less interested in the shells than in the panorama of the ruined town, the littered beaches under the summer sun, the sunken ships' masts and funnels sticking out of the calm blue sea, when, suddenly, CRASH!—three or four shells had hit us.

'I was down the tower in a moment. The big stair-case under the front entrance door was blown in. Men were lying under stones and iron gratings, and it seemed they must all be killed. But no one was much hurt and we got them all out on stretchers to the back of the building. The urgent necessity was to move the ambulances, and I managed to get all those in front of the building round the back. I had just finished doing so when the barrage began to envelope the garden. One of the officers and myself dived under one of a group of lorries. The shells were all around, but no one was hit, though every lorry was wrecked to a greater or lesser degree.

'The bombers were also busy. They did not land any in the garden, but very close, not to be wondered at as French AA guns were firing from positions all around us. During the day many wounded Frenchmen crawled in from the fight just up the road.

Our staff bandaged them, and I took them to the French hospital at the brewery. Along the canal road, and even in our garden, the machine-gun and rifle bullets droned overhead, but seemed to be all just safely high.

'Among the lorries left in the grounds was an ammunition waggon. I took this up the road a bit, along the railway, and burnt it in a field. We also destroyed what rifles etc. we could find, and buried them, and any other time to spare I was helping the grave diggers.

'In the later afternoon we were witness to the extinction of a little French Fort between Dunkirk and Zudcoote, which had been holding out. The planes swooped in continuous waves, silencing gun after gun, till only one remained, still hammering away at them. A flight of thirty Stukas dropped their loads, and the last Fort was silenced.

'Towards the evening there was a lull. After doing what could be done for the wounded, the staff sat down in the cellar to the best food we could find, and plenty of red wine from the Chateau cellar. Someone got out a concertina, but no one had the heart to sing. It seemed so very likely we should not be wanting any breakfast. The wireless was on, with a most improbable communique about the Germans not coming any nearer, evacuation proceeding etc. If not so tragic, it would have been funny.

'Outside the French were trying to improvise last minute defences round our gate, and with the greatest difficulty we persuaded them not to dig in actually inside our grounds. They would not be convinced that the hospital had anything to gain by being clear of combatants, being absolutely sure that we should certainly be shot down, wounded and all. It was a depressing forecast, but one I did not share, as by this time I was quite certain that the bombers had spared the hospital as far as they could with the guns all round. Anyhow, I went to bed in the cellar, and slept the clock round.

'Sometime before 8 o'clock, I got up, and as soon as I was

outside, I met the Germans, who were walking up the drive.

'There were a handful of infantrymen with their tommy guns and hundreds of rounds of ammunition, and a few yards behind a middle-aged Red Cross man with a bicycle. They were as fresh as paint, washed and shaved, in fact it later appeared that they had rested in their lines for the night, leaving the remainder of the French troops to clear out of the town towards the docks, blow up the last bridge, and prepare, on the wide, open plain to which I have referred, a last stand. This saved any street fighting and, by allowing the Germans to walk quietly in and not fight their way, probably saved our lives. None of us put up our hands or did any "Kamerad" stunt, and from the first they behaved in an entirely correct manner towards the hospital. After looking for French stragglers in the garden, whom they frightened out of their wits but did not shoot, they set a guard on the gate and went on, leaving a few Red Cross personnel only to look after us.'

Following on his graphic description of the evacuation and the fall of Dunkirk, Gaze's account of the immediate aftermath comes inevitably as something of an anti-climax. He records with admiration the courage and cheerfulness of the badly wounded British troops, for whom everything possible was done, with meagre resources, by a small, largely untrained staff. The operating theatre was kept busy, with many gangrened limbs amputated. One blood-chilling hospital episode stands out. It seems to sum up the whole macabre business of war, its savagery, its belittlement of human life, its twisted values.

'The stray dogs, which had sheltered from bombs and shellfire in the comparative security of the hospital, began to develop a most unpleasant taste for the bloody dressings on the ground. They licked them and would soon have begun on other things with blood on them, so I killed several of them. The officers got to hear of it and, being animal lovers, objected to my iron bar and ordered the next dog into the operating theatre.

'After a very considerable waste of cocaine, ether and other drugs, which the creature seemed to enjoy, I had it given back to me to deal with, and after that no questions were asked. As a matter of fact, one of the Germans showed me a very humane way of despatching a dog.'

2 *Retreat from Abbeville*

'After resting we pressed on, but owing to our exhausted condition we had to make frequent stops to rest. The starting-off process after such a rest was torture owing to our feet. I thought of the Retreat from Mons, and said to the others that nobody could appreciate a retreat until one had taken part in one.'

The date is Wednesday, 22 May 1940, and Company Quarter-Master Sergeant J. S. Brown, laden with rifle and pack, is stumbling in the rain along the road to Rouen in a stream of French and Belgian refugees. There are three other sergeants and three privates with him, but they have no idea what has become of the rest of their company. They do not even know how close are the pursuing Germans, whose bombers have already left Abbeville and Dieppe palled in black smoke.

John Brown, a solicitor's clerk serving in a Territorial battalion before call-up, was just another number in the British Expeditionary Force, whose short-lived stand against the German blitzkrieg takes up little space in the war histories. But for him it was an experience he did not mean to forget. Throughout the eight weeks in which he was caught up in the chaotic retreat from Abbeville to Cherbourg he kept a daily record of everything that happened. As one reads the neatly penned entries in his little grey notebook, he comes stolidly alive—a Yorkshire type, phlegmatic, stoical, a stickler for Duty, but sharply observant of the shortcomings of his superiors. ' . . . We took up a defensive position. The position was a poor one with a field of fire of only about 50 yds. Also if fire was brought to bear some boys would have fired on others . . . '

In parts the diary reads as stiffly as an official report painstakingly penned in an Orderly Room. But gradually a nightmare air of unreality sets in. '. . . There were dead people, men, women and children, scattered at the side of the train. The engine driver had his head off. There was a dog sitting mourning by a dead man . . .' He is escaping in frantic circles, nobody seeming to know what is going on. The Enemy is breathing down his neck but never shows his face.

That the diary was in fact jotted down as events happened is clear towards the end. Brown's pen splutters as he is writing the name 'Creully' because, as he briefly explains, a German plane flew machine-gunning along the Normandy road at that moment. And there is no doubt that it was very soon after he had finally thrown off his equipment and collapsed on the deck of a troopship in Cherbourg harbour that he recorded the fact. For the first time in the 12,000-word diary, the handwriting is shaky. Like the writer, it leans sideways and comes off the lines.

The diary starts on 25 April when the King's Own Yorkshire Light Infantry were given an enthusiastic send-off from Dewsbury Station, Yorkshire. They sailed from Southampton in one of six transports, convoyed by a destroyer and met by French planes nearing Cherbourg. From 28 April to 18 May Brown was in a Nissen hut camp at Montreuil in the Pas de Calais area, waiting on events.

It is glorious weather and he goes for tramps through the countryside with Dick and Sgt Holroyd and Sgt Potter, splits a bottle of champagne at supper in an estaminet, attends a camp concert, goes on a distant trip to Rennes which he finds 'spacious and clean with its canal and bridges like Venice'. On 13 May the camp learns that Germany has invaded Holland, Belgium and Luxemburg, and there are orders that steel helmets, respirators and gas capes are to be carried when out of camp.

But war is still remote. That night Brown hears nightingales in a nearby wood. Next day the sergeants beat the officers at football, 4 to 1. And it is with no premonition of what is to come that he describes, with unwonted lyricism, a walk back to camp with friends from a village cafe. 'It was splendid tramping over the rough roads with sparks flying from hob boots and a crescent moon just over the woods on our right and close to it a brilliant star.'

Then, on 18 May, they entrain in cattle trucks and, cheered by thousands as they pass through wayside stations, rumble slowly along the congested lines towards the nightmare. Two days later they are on their way from Dieppe to Abbeville.

'*Monday, 20 May, 1940*. All day we passed train after train full of Belgian troops with artillery and machine guns travelling in opposite direction to us. They grinned at us and made gestures of throat cutting pointing in the direction we were going. Everyone wondering what it all meant. Also passed a Hospital Train full of wounded, some being women and little children. 4 pm. Orders given to leave train and take to wood at side of railroad. Hun planes came over us and dropped bombs on some place over the woods to the right. Two planes were shot down. After raid, boarded train and proceeded. On moving out of woods could see a great deal of smoke in the distance. Smoke becomes much nearer as train proceeds.

'Arrived just outside Abbeville Station at 4.30 pm. Abbeville on fire. As train stopped somebody shouted out "Look, parachutists", and on looking in the direction indicated saw several aircraft approaching the train from across the Somme, and the parachutists were AA shells. We grabbed equipment and rifles and took cover at the side of the train. About forty enemy planes came over and bombed Abbeville unmercifully. The machines were very high indeed and AA fire had no effect on them. Several bombs dropped not very far from us. Raid lasted half an hour and after boarding the train and being in for a few minutes eighteen planes came over. Took cover between the train and the Somme. Town again bombed without mercy. During the raid refugees fled along the banks of the Somme from Abbeville.

'After raid over the Battalion fell in. Heavy artillery fire could be heard east of Abbeville. Whilst being fallen in on the banks of the Somme we had constantly to open our ranks to allow civilians to pass through. It was pitiful to see them. Old men, women of all ages, and young children, with a few belongings. One girl about eighteen years of age passed through our ranks laughing wildly. She was alone and had a mad expression on her face. Another woman about twenty-five years of age was led by an elderly woman also in black. She looked broken in spirit and heart. I wondered if she were a widow who probably lost her child in the bombardment. It seemed so strange to me to see on one side a beautiful summer day with birds singing and the river moving gently by, and on the other a blazing town, with dense black smoke issuing from it.

'All ranks were carrying packs and the Battalion moved off by platoons at intervals except HQ Coy. I lead HQ Platoon of the Coy, and followed at the rear of the Coy. About a kilo up the Somme we had to take cover under the trees on account of a further raid. French troops on other side of the river also moving away. Hun planes came over town again and bombed. After they had cleared away we moved off, and on arriving about 100 yards from the Bridge over Somme about two kilos from Abbeville we halted owing to Bridge being congested by vehicles. Whilst waiting to move off I kept scanning the sky. About this time I heard heavy artillery fire in the east, but no shell bursts, denoting that the artillery was AA. After a few minutes I saw eighteen Hun aircraft in formation very high and gave orders for my Platoon to take cover. The Platoon ahead did not take cover and I shouted and ordered them to do so. After they had taken cover I noticed that the Platoon at the Bridge head had not taken cover, and I shouted and ordered them to cover. I then walked to the two Platoons. I discovered that the Platoon immediately in front of me had no Platoon Commander so I assumed command of it. The Platoon at the Bridge head was commanded by 2/Lt Aykroyd, and I told him that I had taken command of the Platoon to his rear. I also commented to him on the heavy artillery fire in the East, but he thought it was AA. I pointed out the lack of shell bursts in the sky. The raiders passed over us and bombed Abbeville again.

'We then moved forward and crossed the Bridge in single file at intervals. The road on the other side was congested with traffic, cars, carts, trucks, lorries and civilians, and we had to force our way through them. Whilst doing so we had to take cover again owing to a further flight of bombers. When they had passed we moved into a field on the right of the road and took cover under the trees which bordered the field. My feet were beginning to become sore, and my equipment was very heavy. Also my water-bottle was empty and I had not had a drink since early morning, consequently I was very thirsty. Whilst we waited there I spoke to Joe about the heavy artillery fire, and he agreed with me that it was artillery fire. Joe also agreed with me in the opinion that we were in a sticky position. Mr Aykroyd came to me and enquired if I had my prismatic compass, and I told him I had left it at home. He then detailed a reconnoitring patrol, and I enquired where they were to go, and was informed they were going to ascertain the Enemies' position. Another big flight of bombers passed over us and bombed Abbeville whilst we were at this spot.

'About 7 p.m. we moved off out of the field, crossed the road and passed across two or three fields where we took up a defensive position. The position was a poor one with a field of fire of only about fifty yds. Also if fire were brought to bear some boys would have fired on others. On moving up to take our position I saw some of the REs who had accompanied us on the train, and they had a Lewis gun with them. I wondered what the outcome of the night would be. After being there for a few minutes orders were received to move to the fields to the north of that position. On arriving at our new position we faced the east and lined a dry shallow ditch. The field of fire in this position was very limited.

'I laid down here and after a short while Capt Phythian sent word down to me to join him. I reported to him, and he told me that he wanted me to remain near to him. I brought my Platoon up to him, and we rested there. By this time the moon, a full one, had risen. The artillery fire had also increased in intensity, and we could also hear the fire of automatic weapons. At 9 pm Capt Phythian, who had been speaking to the CO, came to me and said we were moving off back to the railway where a train was waiting for us. He said we were to move in single file and that I had to keep close behind him.

'We reached the road which was congested with vehicles, civilians and troops, and crossed the Bridge over the Somme. We then inclined right and moved northwards between the river and the railway. We halted there to get all the Coy together, and whilst we rested we were informed that German tanks had entered Abbeville. By this time it was dusk, but the light was good owing to the brilliant moon. We moved off again in single file at the right side of the railway track. The going was very rough owing to the big stones which had been laid as ballast. Also dozens and dozens of big petrol drums lined the side of the track for several hundred yards, which made progress difficult. Capt Phythian pressed us to take a very quick pace. By this time I was exhausted by my heavy equipment and pack, and thirst and sore feet were troubling me.

'Sgt Wall the Intelligence Sgt passed us on a cycle going northwards and Capt Phythian shouted and enquired about the train. Sgt Wall replied he was going to see about it. We then came upon our French Intelligence Officer who told us the train was ahead and we were to make for it. Sgt Wall passed us again going this time in the direction of Abbeville. Capt Phythian asked him where the CO was, and then told me he was going back to speak to him. He told me to carry on. I pressed on panting, and only the thought of home kept me going.

'Three or four miles from the Bridge over the Somme we came to a level crossing where I met some of our HQ men. We passed on until we arrived at a Bridge which was full of troops, both British and Belgian. Two British Officers were there and they asked for the Sgt Major in command. I told them I was in command, and they told me they had a German spy whom they desired to hand over to me. I told them that I could not take the spy off their hands, and also told them what my orders were. There was a train with saloon carriages full of passengers alongside us and I enquired if this was our train. One of the officers said the train was full of refugees and that it was not moving off for two days. He also said that the train could not go very far owing to the line being up. He said they were getting rid of their equipment and hiking it and advised me to do likewise.

'Whilst talking I saw the light of a train about 100 yards ahead. We made for the train which was moving at a walking pace and came up to the last truck. There were troops in front of us who leaped on to the trucks. My party jumped on to the last truck which contained boxes. There were also a number of troops in the truck whom I ascertained were Belgians. The men with me who had got in the truck were L/Cpl Ward, Pte Norbury, Pte R. Ball, Pte L. Ball, Pte Cowley, and another man whose name or Coy I did not know. A moment or so after boarding the truck several Belgian soldiers came alongside the truck and asked for me. They said that the British Officers had sent the "Bosche Espion" to me. I told the Belgians that I could not deal with the spy and they enquired what they had to do with him. I told them to shoot the spy.

'It then occurred to me how it was known that this man was in fact a spy, so I enquired if he had been tried. The Belgians replied in the negative, and I told them not to shoot him. I also said that as their force was greater than mine they had better take the spy. They took him into the next truck. I looked out of the truck which was moving very slowly, but could not see anybody following the train. I did not know whether there were any of our Battalion on the train, and I shouted out and enquired. I did not get any reply.

'We had a conference as to what steps we should take next, and I wanted to get out and make our way back towards Abbeville in the hope of contacting the Battalion. The remainder were against this course, and under the circumstances I did not feel justified in insisting on this step. Whilst we discussed the situation several engines passed us going in the direction of Abbeville, but we could not ascertain whether they had trucks or carriages attached. In view of this traffic the idea of leaving the truck and going back was not feasible, and I abandoned it. It was decided that we would remain in the truck until morning when we would alight and wait for our own people coming up the line. In the event of missing our Battalion I decided that we would make our way to the sea, moving at night and hiding by day, and act as a fighting patrol.

'The Hun planes came over the train several times bombing, and we could hear the distant explosion of bombs. After being in the train about half an hour, during which time it travelled about three or four kilos, it stopped just outside a station. Whilst we stood there the engine with coaches passed us at a slow speed. I stood in the doorway of the truck, shouting out as each coach passed "Are there any KOYLIs on board?" I also flashed my torch on the windows. A voice from one coach shouted "Yes". This gave me great hope. Our engine went on and we passed the coaches again and I repeated my enquiries and got a second response.

'A short distance further on the engine stopped again, and we ascertained that the signal lights were against us. One of the Belgian soldiers could speak good English, and he told us that he was born in England in 1916 whilst his parents were refugees. He stated that the Belgian troops were going to Paris and from there to the south of France for training. The train had not moved for some time and it was suggested that probably the enemy were in possession of the controls of the signals, and had put them at 'stop'. This was a possibility, and we got ready to leave the train if necessary.

'After the train had been stopped about half an hour, a Belgian Officer came to the truck and ordered the Belgian troops out. Prior to this I should mention that a commotion occurred in the next truck to us and after it subsided two Belgian soldiers climbed into the truck we were in, and on enquiring about the noise was informed that the Spy was giving trouble. We alighted from the truck with the Belgians, and I noticed that when the Belgians alighted from the next truck they did not bring the spy out with them.

'We moved up the railway line for three or four hundred yards where we came to a level crossing. The Belgians passed out on to the road to the left of the crossing, where they appeared to be falling in. I enquired the reason for leaving the train and was told that the line was up further on. I found the Belgian Officer who could speak French and a little English, and I enquired if there were any British troops with his men. He told me that I could find some further up the road. Two or three hundred yards up we came upon a party of REs. I asked if there were any KOYLIs with them and was told there was a party several hundred yards ahead. We pushed on ahead and came upon Mr Knott, Mr O'Connor, RSM McCarthy, RQMS Burton, Sgt Snowden and about twenty ORs. I reported to Mr O'Connor and we fell in with them.

'After travelling some distance I had to abandon my pack, just taking some socks, handkerchiefs, a tin of cigarettes, ground sheet and my hairbrush and case and balaclava helmet. I was in a very bad state on account of thirst and had difficulty in speaking. At the rear left of us we could see the glare of burning Abbeville, and enemy bombers were nearly constantly passing overhead. We stopped at a cross-roads where I lay on my back in the wet grass. Mr O'Connor borrowed my map which he studied under a ground sheet.

'After a short while we came upon the railway again which we followed. Whilst travelling along the line we came upon a wrecked ambulance train. The train appeared to have been bombed and machine gunned. There were dead people, men, women and children, scattered at the side of the train. The engine driver had his head off. There was a dog sitting mourning by a dead man. A small ambulance car had toppled off the train and lay in the road on its roof. Steam was hissing from the engine. It was a horrible sight.

'We passed on and came upon some refugees. Mr O'Connor carried the suit case for one of the refugees for some distance, but our pace was quicker than theirs and we passed them. The thirst was horrible and had become a torture. It was with the greatest effort of will power that I did not kneel down and drink from the puddles of water in the muddy track. Finally the RSM observed my distress and gave me his water bottle to drink from. It was a god-send and I could have drunk the bottleful. I drank a little and carried the bottle for him.

'Just before dawn we came to a metalled road and about 7 am we arrived at a village where we rested. I saw a cafe there and went to obtain water, which I required badly. The people at the cafe refused to give me water, and finally I bought a syphon of soda water for which I was charged 50 Frs. We left the village and about 9 am reached another village where we rested in a footpath just off the main road. Immediately I laid down I fell into a coma, from which I was aroused before we moved off. I was then dead beat, and RQMS Burton gave me a drink of whisky from his flask. He also told me that it was hoped that transport could be obtained a little further on.

'We walked a short distance when we met a truck with Capt Taylor on board. Two other fellows and myself were put on board, and we were taken to Eu about three or four miles distance. I don't remember anything about the journey there.

On arriving at Eu we were put off and went to the CMP camp where we had tea, biscuits and jam. News was received that the enemy were close and the CMP packed and left. Whilst we waited for the truck to call for us I saw two enemy AFVs some 500 yards away. Several enemy aircraft came but did not bomb or machine gun us.

'*Tuesday, 21 May.* Capt Taylor returned with the truck about mid-day and we left Eu at about 12.30 pm with the intention of travelling to Dieppe. On our way we had to warn a RASC camp of the close proximity of the enemy. The RASC packed immediately and we left in convoy for Dieppe. We stopped on a road running through a thick wood, where the RASC had some food. We then took a roundabout road to Dieppe which we reached at 4 pm. It was decided by the Convoy Commander to take the Convoy through to Rouen so Capt Taylor and our party alighted. We walked to the Harbour, and Capt Taylor left us to find transport to take us to a Camp on the outskirts of Dieppe. We remained against the Bridge.

'At 4.30 pm a number of aircraft came over from the direction of the sea. There was no AA fire and I thought the planes were French or ours. My first information that they were enemy aircraft was two violent explosions, one on the Hospital Ship *Maid of Kent* which was moored about 100 yds from us. A big piece of stone thrown up by a bomb splinter struck me on my right knee and I was knocked down. We took cover at the side of the Bridge. In front of me lay a French officer and another one fell nearly on me. A number of bombs were dropped. The only return fire was from LMGs made by French soldiers, but the planes were far too high for the fire to be effective.

'After dropping their load of bombs, the planes cleared off. We got up and moved back to the Bridge. The *Maid of Kent* was on fire and a huge column of black smoke was issuing from it. Another place was also on fire beyond the *Maid of Kent*. A Hospital train on the quayside had its rear coaches on fire. A piece of bomb casing had gone through the window of the Cafe near to which we had sheltered, and a girl had been struck by splinters all over her face and neck. A small boy about eight years of age had been hit in the ankle. Wounded and sick men were on the *Maid of Kent,* and they were carried off. A few minutes later a second batch of enemy planes came over and bombed. This time we took shelter under the bank of the river. After the raid was over we came from our shelter, but we were driven back by another flock of enemy bombers. The raids lasted until 5.30 pm.

'Capt Taylor came back about 5.45 pm and after discussing the matter it was decided that we would get transport to Rouen. He arranged for transport in a convoy just leaving for Rouen and we got in a truck. The *Maid of Kent* was then sinking fast and still on fire. The wounded were being transferred on to the Hospital train, and we were held up until the train moved off. We left for Rouen about 6 pm and on passing the Military Hospital we saw where a bomb had struck the Lodge. We later heard that the Hospital itself had been bombed and machine gunned, and that some of our fellows were in it at the time.

'About a kilo out of Dieppe we met the CO, Mr Knott and Mr O'Connor. The lorry was stopped and the CO told us that the Battalion was reforming on the ridge above the railway where we had had breakfast the previous morning. We got off the lorry and joined 80 to 100 of the Battalion against the station two kilos from Dieppe. I enquired for 'B' Coy but with the exception of a few fellows who had straggled in there were none, and no information regarding their whereabouts. The CO said he was going to arrange for some food and transport for us, and we waited there. About 8 pm many of the men became very anxious and restive and several began to leave us and got on transport going out of Dieppe. The officers with us were Mr Coles and another whose name I don't know. There was ample transport to have got the men away, but nothing was done.

'In the meantime Capt Taylor had gone to Dieppe to find the CO and he returned a few minutes before 9 p.m. and said he had been unsuccessful. At 9 pm we were given orders to get to Rouen as best we could, and we marched off in sections at intervals. With me there were Bugle Major Hubert, Sgt Potter, Sgt Holroyd, Pte Norbury, Pte Bell and another man whom I did not know. Night fell, with heavy clouds which shielded the moon. We did not know the road, had no map or compass, the only information we had was that the enemy was somewhere on our left flank and that he was expected to occupy Dieppe that night.

'It soon became apparent that the remainder had not taken the road we were on. A convoy of British troops overtook us, and I stopped it and enquired if it was going to Rouen. I was told that the convoy was going to the front line at Le Treport, and I asked if we could go with them. I was in that condition that I would have gone anywhere provided I could ride. The Officer in command gave us permission, but when the others knew where the convoy was going they refused to go. We therefore marched on.

'We stopped at one or two cafes and asked them to fill our waterbottles, but they refused to do so. We also had a rest by a wayside Calvary, and whilst there I made a silent prayer for home and family. I intended further lightening my equipment at this point, but the others, who did not realise how far away Rouen was and thought we could walk it by morning, desired to push on, and I did not get the chance to do so. We fell in with two Belgian civilians who could speak English. One of them carried my rifle for a distance. They told us they were officers in the merchant service, and that their ship had been lost owing to enemy action. Whilst with them we stopped at another estaminet and asked for water for our bottles, and were refused. The two Belgians spoke to the patron and insisted that water be provided, and at last we got our bottles filled. This was a great relief to me because I dreaded the agony of thirst I had suffered the evening and night previously. We were losing a great deal of moisture from our bodies owing to perspiration with which we were constantly drenched.

'The road had a constant procession of vehicles of every description and age, together with men, women and children on foot and Belgian and French soldiers. About midnight we decided to rest at the side of the road, and have a little food. I provided a tin of bully and a packet of biscuits. Sgt Hubert had a tin of sausages and a loaf of French bread, and we had a meal. We decided to have a short sleep and rolled ourselves in our gas capes. I awoke at 2 am owing to the bitter cold. I heard bombers passing over and bombs were dropped in the direction of Dieppe. The others woke up and I produced some chocolate which we ate whilst we prepared to move. I changed my socks. My feet were in a shocking state, blistered, the skin off in several places and my toes were bleeding. My right knee was also very stiff and painful.

'The road was much quieter at this hour and rain began to fall. We marched for about 2½ hours, and then had to rest in a cart road off the main road. We got what shelter we could under some trees, but the rain became very heavy indeed. We rested there despite the rain until we had recovered a bit, and then I made a reconnaissance down the cart road which led to a farm. I found a barn, and went back and led the others to it. We lay down on the floor and slept until 5.30 am.

'*Wednesday, 22 May.* I got up and went to the farmhouse which was occupied. I asked to buy food, but they said they had neither bread nor eggs to sell. I saw some milk so I bought seven basinsful. I roused the others and brought them to the farm-house where we drank the milk. It was still raining very heavily. I took off my cartridge carrier and after placing the cartridges in a bandolier, I dumped the carrier and some books into a stream. We then set off. Our feet were so bad that we could only shuffle along. The streams of refugees and Belgian soldiers came along the road which became as congested as ever. My stomach began to give me trouble and I felt very sick and ill. About 10 am we came to a village from which people were evacuating, and we called at an estaminet and had a bottle of vin blanc with which we ate the remainder of the bread and a tin of bully I had carried. I also had my flask filled with cognac.

'After resting we pressed on, but owing to our exhausted condition had to make frequent stops to rest. The starting-off process after such a rest was torture owing to our feet. I thought of the Retreat from Mons, and said to the others that nobody could appreciate a retreat until one had taken part in one. One stop was made on a bridge over a swift running stream which was nearly overflowing its banks owing to the heavy rainfall. We lay on the wet pavement on the bridge and rested. The country was very beautiful, with hills and woods. Sgt Holroyd was very much afraid that the enemy would overtake us, and would not let us take proper rest. We pushed on and at midday came to a barn at the side of the road. We went inside and lay in deep straw. I took off my boots and socks, and washed my feet with water from my water bottle. I then dressed them with my First Field Dressing.

'Sgt Hubert, Sgt Potter and myself were for spending the remainder of the day and night here, and setting off the next day, but Sgt Holroyd had the breeze up and could see enemy tanks passing the barn. We pulled his leg, but his state influenced the younger soldiers. We left the barn at 2 pm and after a short distance came to a cafe where we bought some tins of peas and tomatoes, two cups of coffee each, and a big bag of lump sugar which was very sustaining. We had a few words at this point with a French ambulance worker who told us that as far as he knew the enemy had not occupied Dieppe. We marched on and in the late afternoon when about 15 kilos from Rouen I knew I could not carry on any further and became desperate.

'I told the others that we were going to stop cars and put two men on mudguards. The next car to come along was stopped at the rifle point and two men placed on the mudguards. I did this until only Bell and myself were left. We then stopped a car and got on the mudguards. The car travelled about 100 yds and then stopped, the driver telling us that he had run out of petrol. We walked on for a distance and stopped another car which we boarded. This car only took us a matter of 20 yds before it stopped for lack of petrol. We walked on, and when about 10 kilos from Rouen I stopped a lorry carrying refugees and requested a lift. Although the lorry was full they consented. I had to be lifted on to the lorry. I hadn't the strength to get on. The people on it were Belgians, and one a girl about 18 years of age could speak good English and she told us they were from Brussels. They were very kind to us indeed.

'We arrived at Rouen at 8 pm and reported to the Garrison WOs and Sgts' Mess where we had a bath, shave and a meal. Owing to our condition we were permitted to sleep the night at the Mess, and I had a bedroom with a real bed. I went to bed at 9 pm and was sound asleep immediately I lay down.'

Next day, a lovely sunny day marred only by air raid warnings and distant shellfire, Brown was back to desk duty, preparing an Acquittance Roll to pay out what remained of the Battalion, when the Camp Commandant summoned all CQMSs and asked for two volunteers to go to a forward area as Brigade QMSs. 'I felt it my duty to go and put up my hand', he writes.

Brigade HQ was in a village château and there he learned that they were to be 'a last barrier against the Hun, a fight to the finish'. When reinforcements arrived the position became less precarious but for the two weeks Brown spent here and in a subsequent château he was only vaguely aware of the fluctuations of the fighting. German bombers, some with French markings, frequently came over, dropping not only bombs but saboteurs and spies and Brown took part in parachutist patrols in nearby woods. Refugees continued to stream through. Time bombs shook the château. 'To think that a lovely hot summer's day with blue skies and a lovely countryside should be subject to this treatment.' Then, on 7 June, the diary has an entry that suggests the emotions he has bottled up inside him. He describes what happened as 'a startling change of heart which I am glad to note, which proves conclusively that war has not deprived me of human kindness'.

'At 4.15 pm a French or British fighter attacked a Messerschmitt 109 just at the side of the Château. At 4.30 I was in the Orderly Room when in walked a German airman accompanied by one of our Privates. He was carrying an automatic pistol in a holster and I took it off him. The right side of his face was cut and he had been grazed by a bullet at the base of the skull. He was shaken up very badly and trembling. I sent for the Adjutant and the MO and got him a chair to sit on. My heart which I thought was cold and pitiless turned to water at the sight of him. I gave him a cigarette and a drink of rum from my flask. He told me he was the pilot of the Messerschmitt, shot down a kilo away.

'I took his particulars. His name was Hauptmann Bernhard Mielks, born Dortmund on 21-4-13 and he produced his identity card. He told me he had fought in Spain for Franco. The MO came and dressed his wounds and I enquired if he had any cigarettes. He said he hadn't so I gave him a packet of twenty Abdullas. Before he was taken away he gave me his knife, a splendid affair, for a souvenir. He looked a splendid chap. You can admire a fighter pilot.'

But at 10 pm that night Brown is recording 'Hell on earth. Forges blazing in the east. Got everything packed and ready stood by. CO orders that we shall maintain our position through the night and retire tomorrow if necessary. All horizon from north-east to south alight with flashes from shell fire and bombs. This is the worst night of my life with the exception of the Abbeville retreat. Lay on my bed thinking about home and whether I would ever see it again. Couldn't sleep owing to the noise. All the civilians have evacuated. War is a wicked, insensate thing.

'8 June. Woke 4 am. Guns silent, no bombing. Got up and washed and shaved. Break of another lovely hot day. Pall of smoke lies over what remains of Forges. Poor Forges. Everything seemed hushed and quiet. Went for a walk around. Cows, new born calves, sheep and lambs, pigs, poultry, rabbits left behind at château when evacuated. Men let them loose and turned them into fields. 2 pm. Orders to burn all papers and put kits on trucks. 7 pm. Gunfire and bombing. The whole eastern sky-line one pall of smoke from burning villages and towns. Orders to retire.'

For the next ten days Brown was almost constantly on the move on mostly congested roads harassed by German planes. He reached as far as Le Mans only to be sent back to the 'line' near Rouen, where he was billeted one night in a 'pretty black and white cottage with "RF 1786" carved on a wooden beam, roses in bloom round doorway and at side of house honeysuckle'. On the way to Rouen his convoy was warmly greeted by the streams of refugees. 'They all put their thumbs up to us even the tiny kids. Girls by the hundred in the towns and villages waved and threw kisses to us. It is because we are going back to the front. If we had been going in the opposite direction they would not have looked at us.'

The refugees were a sight Brown would not forget. 'It is pitiful to see the poor women and children. We passed one woman with two boys and two girls. The little girls were carrying their dollies. Another mother was washing the sore feet of a little boy at a wayside stream. These sights hurt me more than anything else. Women and children should not be subjected to such horrors and hardships.'

By 16 June Brown was at Honfleur in Normandy. 'Woken 4 am by barrage. Great fear that French will capitulate and that we shall be taken prisoners. Took Holy Communion at 8 am service outside farmhouse with small table for altar. Received a great deal of consolation from it. The guns were silent during the service and a bird sang beautifully. Worked all morning on lists of missing men. 500 missing at moment. 2 pm. Letters from Janet. Very excited, and nearly afraid to open them.'

Monday, 17 June, was to be the last stage in the nightmare retreat.

'We are all tired and nerve wracked. I have not had twelve hours sleep since a week last night. 8 am. Orders to move immediately. Passed through Caen, Creully, Bayeux, to cross-roads where we stopped. At 12.30 Hun twin engined bomber came along at about 100 feet going in direction of Cherbourg. He didn't bomb or machine gun. As I had reached the first 'l' in 'Creully' when writing this up the same Hun or his pal came down the road again machine gunning this time. We are on our way now to Cherbourg to embark for home, and it looks that the Hun intends to make our last journey in France an exciting one, and if possible our last journey.

'Road packed with army vehicles, guns, Bren carriers and DRs all going in direction of Cherbourg. 20 kilos to go when Hun bombers flying low came along machine gunning, got into ditch but planes too fast to attempt shot with rifle. Then several minutes later they returned along road. Stuck up owing to traffic jam. Hot, boiling hot afternoon. Orders to fall in and march. 5 pm. Took up defensive position outside Cherbourg. Streams of troops and motor transport going down hill into town. 6 pm. News that French have capitulated and that we had twelve hours to get out of country from 2 pm today.

'7.15 pm. Orders to fall in and march into Cherbourg, Mr Griffiths, RQMS Coombe and myself at the rear of the Battalion. Very exhausted and feet, which have not recovered from the last march, giving out. Marched at ease through the town. People watched us pass through. There was no cheering. Then to the docks. As we crossed some open ground to the boat Hun aircraft came over, machine gunning. I was too tired, footsore and exhausted to look up at them or even care whether I was hit or not. At last on board a crowded ship. Off with equipment and collapsed on deck. Sweat right through clothing.

'Left Cherbourg at 9.45 pm. Harbour full of troopships loading men as fast as possible and getting away. Finally assisted below and had feet attended to. News that U-boats were trying to sink troopships. Last glimpse of France in the dusk. Then to bunk where fell asleep. Woke up at 1.30 am, thought light of electrics was sunlight and couldn't understand where I was. Then pulled myself together and had a good wash and shaved three days' beard off.

'*18 June*. Disembarked at 5 am and went to station. Saw Sgt Spencer who told me what was left of 2/4 Btn was short distance away. Got my kit and went and rejoined. Thirty-four officers and men boarded and one was killed on board.'

At 7 pm that night Brown arrived at Leeds station. He was unable to walk and, after being examined by a Medical Officer, was taken to 28th General Military Hospital. 'In great pain, foot septic,' he ends his diary. 'Cannot believe we are safe and out of the hell of the past weeks. Blessed sleep in a real bed with white sheets.'

3 *Battle Honour in Tunisia*

'I have written this partly to exorcise obsessive memories and partly because I have found very few accounts of infantrymen in the last war that had much resemblance to what I experienced and felt.'

This is the preface to a stark account of what it was like, as a young platoon commander, to be fighting in Tunisia during the last stages of the North African campaign in 1942. John Clark, a schoolmaster since 1950, married with two daughters, must be representative of many ex-servicemen who are still occasionally haunted by memories of war as it actually was. The events he describes—a night patrol, a last-ditch stand, capture by the Germans—are the raw material of many a swashbuckling film scenario or adventure story. Clark leaves them raw. No gloss of heroics. A sense, rather, of confusion, insignificance, impotence, a painful insight into the feelings of an unseasoned young officer faced for the first time with the casualness of killing. Of a corporal in his platoon who was killed while carrying out a hurried order, Clark writes: 'I dare not trust myself to feel his death at the time, but my rage and grief at it fermented in the bottling up and were not purged for years after the war.'

The action took place at a crucial stage of the battle for Tunisia when the Germans had launched three major attacks against the British and Americans. The recently arrived 6th Battalion of the Lincolnshire Regiment, in which Clark commanded the 8th Platoon of A Company, had the task of defending Sedjenane, key point in the enemy's northernmost thrust, a small town on a railway line, with an iron ore mine, set amongst cork forests. The mountainous terrain, churned into mud by torrential rain and constant shelling, had for some time been the scene of bitter and often confused in-fighting. Conditions, indeed, were as different as possible from the still-persisting popular conception of a typical 'Desert War' battlefield.

For Second-Lieutenant Clark, aged 21, son of a Scunthorpe grocer, war had hitherto been mirrored in the OCTU and Battle School training he had undergone since being called up a year before while reading modern languages at St Edmund Hall, Oxford. His initiation was to be brief, undistinguished, but traumatic. And as a prisoner of the Germans for the next two years he had time enough to brood.

Clark has divided his account under seven headings, and, where relevant, has inserted extracts from the battalion's Official History. He wrote it in 1970, primarily, as he says, 'to exorcise obsessive memories' rather than for publication, and it is as factual (down to the obligatory swear-words) as a retentive memory can make it. He starts with a night patrol near Medjez-el-Bab some two weeks before his battalion was moved north to Sedjenane. A man in an earlier patrol had been accidentally shot dead and Clark and his platoon were given orders to fetch back the body.

NIGHT PATROL

'They gave me a guide, a lance-corporal who had been out with the dead man's section. He was exhausted and upset. I was resentful, and so were my men.

' "Why not his own f—— mates? They left him there, the sods."

' "F—— the CO!"

'We put mud on our faces, pulled on our cap comforters and set off. It poured with rain and we lost our way so I decided to go back. Wet, dejected and resentful, I reported to the Company commander who sent me back to the CO. I got a rocket. Officers were not to get lost. So I was to go out the following night accompanied by the company commander and seven platoon. I was to find the body, clear the hamlet, push a patrol towards the German lines and carry the body back. It made me face some of my fears—perhaps the CO intended that, but it also made eight platoon feel singled out for a humiliation inflicted by another platoon in their own company. "Eight platoon—f—— shit platoon!"

'Once again we blackened our faces, put on our cap comforters, and, as soon as it was dark, set off through the minefield. The company commander came with my platoon and seven platoon moved to our left.

'We reached the outskirts of the hamlet about eleven. All was quiet in the moonlight except for occasional bursts of fire, like old sewing machines being cranked—Spandaus in the hills. The company commander and I lay in the mud about 200 yards from the line of bushes on the edge of the settlement. Behind the bushes we could see the rooves of the houses. We had been told that the Germans had a habit of arriving early and waiting for British patrols.

' "Take your platoon and clear those three houses," said the major.

'I could see the Germans waiting with their fingers on the trigger of their Spandau. They had me in their sights and they were leering in anticipation.

' "Go on!" he said.

' "I don't know how to tackle it and I'm not going till you tell me how." I was playing for time.

' "Split into two groups and leapfrog forward ten yards at a time," he said.

'I whispered my orders and we formed an extended line in

two halves. I led one half and my sergeant the other. "Up—run fifteen yards—throw yourself down—into a firing position—watch the others run past you and throw themselves down—then up again . . . "

'We were twenty yards from the bushes and the Germans were laughing. I closed my eyes and ran—waiting for the burst. The branches lashed my face. I opened my eyes. There was no one there.

' "You clear that—you that—you that." The sections moved off. A few minutes later two of the section commanders came back saying that they had cleared the houses. I went to find the third. He was standing with his section behind the bushes at the bottom of the garden. "I'm scared," he said.

'Nothing could be worses than those bushes. I've seen the shot in a score of war films and I still half wince, half laugh when I see it. With a grenade in my pocket and my tommy gun at the ready, I dashed up the path, kicked open the door and found nothing but a table and two chairs which some poor Italian settler had left. The house was empty.

'We moved on through the village and found the body behind a house with chickens picking at its face. It was the first dead body I had ever seen.

'Seven platoon stayed in the hamlet whilst we pushed on with our punishment patrol. We found nothing but a few tank tracks—God knows whether they were British or German. We came back and picked up the stretcher with the body on it.

'Four men took the stretcher and we started back through the mud, changing carriers every hundred yards. I had not realised how slippery the mud was, how heavy a dead body was and how far five miles. I had to do my stint of stretcher-bearing—I had brought the disgrace on the platoon.

'Seven platoon watched us from a distance. They were not allowed to help, it was part of the punishment. How I hated them! They seemed then almost as remote and hostile as the Germans. "Eight platoon—f—— shit platoon . . . "

'The head and shoulders of the corpse kept slipping off the stretcher so I said to my sergeant, "Pull him back on!"

' "I'm a bit sensitive about dead bodies," he said.

'I got hold of the dead man's boots and yanked him back on to the stretcher. He began to slip again. About every four hundred yards I had to yank him back by the boots. My first dead body.'

NIGHT WITHDRAWAL

(from the positions in front of Green Hill to El Ouana on the night of 1 March)

From the Battalion History: 'That night transport came forward and took away all the surplus kit, and the following night the Battalion started back down the road towards El Ouana, leaving in position a platoon from each of the rifle companies to keep the enemy ignorant of what was happening.'

We packed and waited; the rest had gone at eight.
The shelling stopped; the hills were black and
  smothering in the silence.
We stumbled down the goat track: thud of boots,
A belch, a fart and 'F— the f— anti-tank!'
'Let's see if Company have left some loot!'
We crawled into their dug-out, struck a match and found
Three bottles full of whisky, wrapped in tissue paper
  still.
'The f—— Jerries won't get that!'
We swigged it as we walked back down the road.

An hour or two and someone was ahead—
'You eight platoon? We thought you'd had it!'

Down on the grass, feet up, my water bottle out, then
two boiled sweets
And all around the stink of steaming, sweating
khaki serge.

THE HILL

(the Germans attack the Battalion at Sedjenane, 3 and 4 March)

From the Battalion History: 'A report was received that the Foresters had been overrun, and that the enemy were advancing westwards along the road, so urgent steps were taken to complete the defence position. Able Company were placed in position on the right, Baker Company in the area of the station, and Charlie Company along the railway embankment. The CO received verbal orders from the Brigade commander at three o'clock (3 March) to hold Sedjenane at all costs.'

'*3 March.* 6 am. "This will be a great day in the history of the Lincolns," said the colonel. "The Germans have broken through the Foresters and we are the only troops between them and Bone. Today will be a battle honour for the Regiment." The company commander was showing him my position. He had put me half way up a small hillock covered with knee-high bushes. We could see what was going on to our right and left and to our rear but not to our front.

' "What shall I do if they come over the hill at me, sir? We can't see a bloody thing until it is a couple of yards away because of these damn bushes. Shouldn't we be at the top of the hill?

' "You'll have to dart around among the bushes," said the colonel, more important matters on his mind.

' "F—— cowboys and Indians," muttered the mortarman.

'7 am. We were drinking tea and forking bacon out of our mess tins when shouts came from the valley to our right. "Lincolns! The Jerries are here!" A commando patrol was running back with bullets whistling behind them.

'We lay in our coffin slits and watched as the Germans moved along a ridge about a hundred yards to our right. They began to set up mortar and machine gun posts. I told my platoon not to fire unless they spotted us. I was sure that once they knew where we were they would lob grenades at us from the top of the hill without us being able to do much about it.

'9.30 am. The Germans attacked the two platoons behind us who were in position near the road, the railway line and the tunnel. I could see very little from where I was and it was like listening to a very noisy firework display you could not see. Their infantry guns, our mortars and twenty-five pounders and fire from the tanks we had brought up, dropped their offerings behind, to the side and in front of us.

'Smoking would have given our position away so we ate boiled sweets as we listened and watched. Some of our shells and mortar bombs seemed to be dropping closer and closer to our position and one of our tanks about a hundred yards away seemed to be firing at us. Perhaps they had forgotten we were there: perhaps nobody had told them.

'I decided to fire a Very light—the only time in the whole of my short military career that I had felt the need. It was a pretty sight and somebody must have seen it but it seemed to make no difference. Our mortar bombs still fell close. The Germans did not seem interested in us, though they must have seen the Very light. My sense of isolation and impotence increased. I had another boiled sweet.

'2 pm. The attack had come to a halt and the firing had almost stopped. I had had no contact with the rest of the company since early morning. We seemed to be serving very little useful purpose where we were so I told a corporal to send a man back to the company commander to ask if we could withdraw to the main company position.

'A few minutes later there was a shot.

'I waited.

'There was a rustling in the bushes behind me. Two blood-stained hands appeared followed by the thin face of a nineteen-year-old boy in an oversize tin helmet. He belonged to the corporal's section.

' "Corporal went hissen," he said with a bewildered gasp. 'And they gor'im in the back. 'ere. I couldn't do a thing. 'e just bled. Don't know if it was our lot or them. 'e jus' said 'Mary'. That's 'is missus."

'The Corporal was a farm worker from South Lincolnshire. One of the kindest, most courageous and gayest of men.

'6 pm. The company second-in-command appeared carrying a sack full of tins of potatoes.

' "Can I pull back?" I asked. "This is a crazy position." I told him what had happened.

' "No, you've got to stay," he said. "You've put up a good show and the CO is pleased with you."

'He left us the sack. Tinned potatoes were a change after boiled sweets but I broke wind all night.'

From the Battalion History:

3 March: ' . . . All through the rest of the day the Battalion positions were constantly mortared and shelled, gun positions were dive-bombed, and long-range machine gun fire was brought to bear from Point 221 down the railway line. Attacks developed on each of the company positions in turn, but they were all beaten off and by midnight the only casualties were one killed and ten wounded.'

4 March: 'At two in the morning, after an attack by an enemy patrol had been beaten off by Baker Company HQ, a two-company attack was put in and for the rest of the night there was a constant small arms and automatic fire from the station area.'

'2 am. The sand in the trench was damp with the mist and we were waiting full of boiled sweets and tinned potatoes. Then I heard what I had feared. Boots and voices higher up the slope above us. Boots and voices moving down towards us.

'We could see them now about seven or eight yards away to our left. "Siebente Kompanie" someone shouted, and I could hear snatches of conversation in German. They were leaving the hill just above us and dropping down into the valley on our left. I lay there with my finger in the ring of a 0.38 grenade.

'One of them stopped just before he dropped from sight to our left. He looked in our direction with his Mauser at his hip. Crouched in the coffin slit, I pulled out the pin, threw it at the silhouette, then squeezed into the sand and waited.

'There was a flash, an explosion, flying stones and sand, more shots—then silence. I peered over the top of the trench. They were leaving the hill higher up. Perhaps they thought we were not worth winkling out in the dark. Perhaps they did not want to be distracted from their main objective, the station and tunnel behind us.

'A few minutes later the two Vickers guns behind us opened up. We heard shouts, shrieks, running through the bushes. Then, as the bursts of fire became less frequent, the groans and screams of the wounded Germans: "Mutti! Mutti! O Gott! O Gott! . . ."

'3 am. The groans and screams had mostly died away. Then from the valley on our left: "English soldier! I bid you not to shoot. We are come for our blessed comrade."

'A pause. Footsteps coming up the slope to our left. Two figures searching among the bushes where the German with the Mauser had stood. They picked up a body and I nudged my sergeant. We both stood up and pointed our tommy guns at them.

' "You are prisoners!" I said in German.

' "Let me have a go at the buggers," said my sergeant.

' "You can't shoot us," one said in German. "We have just shouted to you that we are coming as stretcher bearers. If you wanted to treat us as soldiers you should have shouted back."

'They were right. I just couldn't mow them down as they stood there arguing with me and holding the body. "Would you like to take him back to our Regimental Aid Post?" I asked. I had no idea where it was, or even if we had one, but I felt that I should make some attempt at scoring a point—or where were the battle honours?

' "No, thank you. Our own Verbandplatz is quite near. It is our company commander. He has been wounded in the lung."

'We walked towards each other. They told me about their families and what part of Germany they came from.

' "Now you know where we are," I said at last, "you might tell your comrades we have let you go and ask them to turn a blind eye when we go."

' "Ja, ja. Das werden wir tun, Herr Leutnant," they said. One of them gave me his desert cap as a souvenir, and off they went with their wounded commander.

' "You should have let me shoot the buggers, sir," said my sergeant. "I haven't shot a Jerry yet."

'4 am. A messenger came from our company commander telling me to withdraw my platoon immediately to the main company area. We scuttled back in the dawn mist by sections with our blankets over our shoulders. There was a mess tin of tea and bacon and biscuits waiting for us, and a place for a smoke.'

CAPTURE

From the Battalion History: 'At three o'clock the withdrawal began, section by section, through woods to the west, and along the edge of the woods parallel to the main road. To cover the withdrawal the tanks fired Besa and smoke on to the village, artillery fired all DFs intense, and a composite platoon of Able and Charlie Companies remained in position, as did the Vickers gunners.'

' "The Hun is round us on three sides," said the company commander, "and he has a Spandau on the Djebel behind us.

We're pulling out at three this afternoon but leave your platoon sergeant and three Bren gunners to cover your withdrawal. They pull out half an hour after the rest."

'Three Bren gunners thirty yards apart, without their number two's to keep them company, the rest of the battalion leaving them, and a regiment of Germans waiting to attack . . . How would they feel about me if I didn't stay with them? The major didn't mind, so my sergeant took the platoon back.

'The rest of the company had gone and we were alone. The three gunners were spaced out behind a small rise and I was below them where I could keep an eye on all three and on what was happening behind us. Our guns pounded the village and the Germans started mortaring. One of the mortar shells set fire to an Arab hut being used as cover by one of the Bren gunners. I heard a yell above the firing. He had been hit. We carried him into a hollow where there was a small pool. The toe cap of his boot had been shot away and his toes were a smashed and bloody mess.

'As we tried to take off his boot and to work out how we could put a field dressing on the end of his foot, a Spandau sprayed the area round the hollow.

' "The buggers have spotted us."

'The wounded man was whimpering and in too much pain to care what happened. The other two looked at me. OCTU and Battle School had never catered for this.

' "If we carry him across that bit of ground we're sitting targets. We could leave him here and that might give us an even chance of getting away. Or shall we pack in and wait until they come? I'll do whatever you think."

'They didn't want to decide either, and it was unfair to ask them. In the end, more through inertia than anything else, we decided to throw our guns into the pool and wait.

'About ten minutes later a Feldwebel from the Hermann Goering Division ran up and looked down at us. He took our field dressings—his own were made of paper. We showed him the slit trenches a few yards away. They were full of the wounded German prisoners the company had brought in the night before. Fortunately the Spandau firing at us had not hit them.'

THE MINE

'The Germans had motor cycles with stretchers attached for evacuating the wounded. Three of us sat on the stretcher and a German major sat on the pillion. We had gone only ten yards when my ears were stopped and my eyes blinded by a mist full of red and yellow lights. I felt detached from my body and remember thinking, "Now I shall find out what happens after death."

'I could see and hear again but I was still dazed. The driver was slumped over the petrol tank, my left ear was singing, blood was dripping down my nose and the German major was hitting me.

'His ear drum had been burst, too, and he was accusing me of knowing that the mine was there and of allowing the motor cyclist to go over it in order to get him killed. How was I to know our pioneers had left mines to delay the German advance? The doings of the rest of the company, never mind Battalion Headquarters, had been a mystery to me for the past three days.

'So there we were: the German motor cyclist with his insides blown out splayed over the handlebars: and an elegant German major punching me in the chest whilst I protested my innocence and wished I could do something to stop the stream of blood tickling my nose and chin.'

THE DEAD AND THE WOUNDED

From the Battalion History: 'During the Sedjenane action the total casualties were 21 killed, 98 missing, and 46 wounded.'

The dead

Wedged with their mates in two-man trenches:
some blue, some green, some bloated up,
and others white, immaculate, dignified.
Behind the matted hair or red-ringed in their khaki
battle dress a neat and single bullet hole.
The padre picked the discs from in among their guts.
I couldn't.

The wounded

Inside the tunnel, near the entrance,
our doctor and the German worked together—
two nodding heads with downturned mouths.
'Up on the table with him.' 'Rauf, schnell!'
Another shattered groin: the testicles their covering
gone
lay pink and bare and smooth like pigeons' eggs.
They put a dressing on him and then they left him in the
group about to die.
'Next up!'
A jagged bloody scoop below the knee.
'Ja, amputieren. Man kann nichts anders.'
No anaesthetic so I gripped his hand
and watched.
He bit his lip: the knife slipped slowly through the flesh:
with delicate respect they placed the amputated limb
among the severed members in the darkest corner.

THE DIVISIONAL DRESSING STATION

'English prisoners were helping at the German divisional field hospital carrying the wounded from the wards to the operating theatre and the dead to the mortuary. The Germans asked me if I would act as interpreter and I agreed. A captured British medical officer was acting as assistant in the operating theatre.

We both lived in the officers' mess and, like the rest of the patients, staff and prisoners, we were issued with a bar of Fry's Chocolate Cream every day.

'We were told that a supply ship had been lying off Bizerta when the forward troops of the First Army reached the outskirts of the port. Some over-optimistic reconnaissance unit had radioed back that Bizerta had been occupied. The supply ship had entered the harbour and been captured with its cargo of Naafi goodies. The consignment of Fry's Chocolate Cream had been sent to the divisional field hospital.

'There was not much interpreting to do so I helped in the operating theatre. The wounded were brought in from the forward dressing stations still sweaty, dusty and with three or four days' growth of beard. One doctor would put an ether mask on them and start dropping ether on to it whilst another tore off the paper field dressing. My job was to hold the man's arm or leg whilst another doctor scooped out what seemed to me inordinately large quantities of flesh from the infected areas round the wound. A clean dressing was put on and the wounded man stayed in this base hospital or was shipped back to Italy or Germany for more detailed attention.

'One day the divisional general paid a visit. The Germans stood to attention. I did the same and left hold of the patient, who rolled off the table. We all, including the divisional general, pretended that nothing had happened. The general soon left. We picked up the man and carried on.

'I asked the British doctor if this method of administering ether was standard operating theatre procedure. He was a Dr Cohen from Glasgow. "Naw. All you hev to doo is make 'em count and wait till they stop." By this time the Germans had accepted him as a competent theatre assistant and I asked if they would mind if he administered the anaesthetic. They agreed and I can still see his great hooked nose over the mask as he said to some Swabian peasant, "Zählen bitte!" The German would start counting: his voice would trail away: then the steak cutters would begin. There was no need for "holders down" and I was out of a job.

'There was more time now to get to know the hospital staff. One day a wounded German was brought in whom some of them knew and they suggested that when he recovered from the effects of the ether we should all pretend that we were in a British field hospital. We agreed and when he opened his eyes after the operation the British doctor and I began giving orders to the Germans, which they obeyed promptly and with a proper respect. I tried to look as officious and masterful as I could, and they whispered to the patient that he was a prisoner and should be careful what he said and did.

'He was completely taken in. And he was even more bewildered when they finally told him that this was, indeed, a German field hospital and that we were the prisoners. It seems an absurd and cruel joke now. At the time it seemed no more absurd than so much else that was happening, like the daily bar of Fry's Chocolate Cream that we munched together after the incident.'

For Clark, after two years as a prisoner of war, mostly in Germany, the position was reversed when he spent some months interrogating German prisoners in England and Egypt with the Political Intelligence Department of the Foreign Office. In October 1946 he returned to Oxford to complete his degree in modern languages.

It was the sheerest coincidence that, during a year he spent as a builders' labourer before starting his career as a school-teacher, the site foreman turned out to be an ex-private of his old battalion, and the concrete ganger he worked under that same lance-corporal who had been sent with him on the night patrol near Medjez-el-Bab to fetch in the body of the soldier accidentally shot.

But the memory of that night, of the sight and feel of his first dead body, has been one of the many hauntingly cruel and absurd memories that have remained with him over the years, and to which he has tried to give a substance and a name. Quite recently, and totally unexpectedly, it came back to him.

'One night I peeped in to my youngest daughter's bedroom and saw that she had slipped back out of her divan bed whilst she was asleep,' he writes. 'I pulled her gently back by her legs and nearly let go with a start as I saw a flopping bundle in khaki serge slipping on a stretcher in the moonlight.'

4 *The Cook's Tale*

'Today I'm the youngest 53 years old in South Bank, in fact the lads call me South Bank's oldest Teddy Boy. I still like dancing, "boozing", singing, laughing, joking, but not fighting, although not long back a supposed tough guy tried to be funny and I knocked him cold with one blow.'

Ted Smith's assessment of himself in contented middle age is just what one might have expected from his exuberant account of four-and-a-half years in the army, mostly as a cook, written in a bold sloping hand, as full of flourishes as it is sparse on punctuation, on sixty-five sheets of foolscap notepaper. A Tees-sider with a rich Middlesbrough accent, shop steward and local celebrity, proud father of five and grandfather of nine, he has got out of life what he got out of the army. 'I have fun and I still have that something that I feel can overcome any task put before me.'

For Private A. E. Smith, 13050469, Army Catering Corps, the war was a bit of a belly-laugh. Even when the bombs were raining down on London and North Africa, when keeping an army marching on its stomach became a nightmare of improvisation, when he himself succumbed to a captured packet of dehydrated sauerkraut and was rushed to hospital, it was the funny side of things he dwelt on. 'Just as one has to be serious,' he writes, 'so we had some real screams at each other's expense—what a life, what a laugh.'

To plunge into his sprawling, extrovert narrative after the tension and drama of so many personal accounts is a salutary corrective to any recorder of war experiences. Smith was in some ways more representative of the British Army than the man who fired shots in anger. One of a shadowy hinterland of non-combatants, his was as likely as not the guffaw in the public bar, the wolf-whistle in the black-out, the grinning face at the ship's rails as the troopship docked.

Smith makes no bones about the 'goings-on' in barracks or camp, and chuckles at the 'Exemplary' written under the heading 'Character' on his discharge certificate. Pilferings are seen as perks, looting as accepted practice, a bit of skirt as fair game. Referring to the Military Brothel in Bone, Algeria, he writes: 'Good looking cooks with ration facilities didn't have to resort to this means of gratification.' Like Chaucer's cook, Private Smith could look after himself.

Though he was to prove an indefatigable 'drummer up' at many a chaotic stage of the North African campaign, it was quite against his own inclinations that he ever did join the army and became a cook. It was in his father's steps he wished to follow. A Woolwich man, his father had served with the Submarine Service during World War I and married his mother, a Durham miner's daughter, aboard HMS *Lucia* in the river Tees. He died from war injuries when Ted was five, and for the widow and her five children it was a hard struggle through the years of the depression.

Ted Smith takes up the story—a story spontaneously written, with few exact dates, that it would be fruitless to annotate and an impertinence to edit, necessary pruning apart.

'I don't need to tell you about the situation in those days—soup queues and Tony Evans the Means Test man—in fact we had nothing, however we managed to survive and lived rough—bare feet—slag tips—walking miles across the beaches nearby winkling and swimming in the river. Then leaving school at 14 and jobs in the docks, going to 3d hops in the local halls, and always bragging about our dad's exploits in the war, exaggerated or not.

'Then it happened—Charles Laughton in 'Mutiny on the Bounty' and my imagination was fired—in fact it is my unfulfilled dream to sail on a four master, fully rigged sailing ship. Anyway a week after seeing the film I joined a ship which took me to St Lucia, Halifax, Nova Scotia, St Lawrence, and on the way back whilst drinking a toast to the then George and Mary for their Silver Jubilee we saw in the distance a huge iceberg—the most beautiful sight I've seen—and then, my dream, a fully-rigged sailing ship went flying by. Was it the *Panir*—I'll never know. Then home and not long after this, at nineteen years of age, I married and was detailed by the Ministry of Employment to start work as a Rigger.

'At the start of the war I tried to join the Navy but was put into a reserved occupation due to colour blindness. However at the time of Dunkirk—and after numerous attempts—I was finally called up into the Army and reported to Dingle Vale, Liverpool, on my 21st birthday, 11 July 1940. After some rigorous training, I was asked—did I know anything about boilers, and sure enough I fell for it, and was told to report to the cookhouse and look after ten Sawyer Boilers. Little did I know then that "my War" was being shaped for me, and twelve months later I returned to Huyton, Liverpool, to do a course on Army Cooking, entailing Dutch ovens, field kitchens and the lot.

'But prior to that I had been posted with a crowd of others to Beckenham, Kent, to join up with the remnants of the various troops from Dunkirk and we were immediately put to work digging a Tank trap around London, on a 50 mile radius, as an invasion was fully expected. Whilst we were here we had a first class view of the Battle of Britain whilst hiding in the Orchards of Kent. One day we witnessed the destruction of the buildings at Biggin Hill Fighter Drome and the bombing of two shelters full of WAAFS by low-flying German fighter bombers, but the next day—"Private Smith" echoed across the grounds of the big mansion, and I was detailed to report to Sgt Smith who was in charge of the cookhouse (no Catering Corps existed then).

'I assisted in loading all the gear into a three tonner and off we went—pots, pans, knives, forks, spoons, bowls and the lot—to an unknown destination, Richmond Barracks, Surrey. We had no sooner arrived than German bombers dived over the place and up to then no German plane had been near Richmond. Off came all of the equipment and straight away I had to set up the Sawyer Boilers and somehow get them lit up and full of water—this before being allotted a place to sleep in one of the huts.

'All the girls in the nearby school near the old Richmond Baths came over wide-eyed with wonder, and somehow, with the aid of an axe and some nearby fences, I had five boilers full of tea, sugared and milked, ready for about 300 men coming in for meals. The other lads who were destined to be cooks somehow managed to rig up some old ovens and a field kitchen and in no time a hot meal was drummed up for all them lads, stewed meat, potatoes and dumplings like billiard balls and the inevitable stewed prunes and custard for afters, but hungry bellies didn't complain and so we gradually settled in.

'It was soon realised that some one had to cook so I then got the job of up at 4.30 am to light not five but ten boilers—five for water—one for Burgoo—one full of eggs or canned bacon or beans—and the others full of spuds peeled the night before. "How the hell do I light these fires in the Blackout?" and a roar from Quarter Master Cowell "If you don't have all that ready for 6.30, Smith, you're on bloody Jankers", and somehow it was ready and all the while bombs going off all over London.

'The place was literally bombed night after night. In particular—on one Friday night—some of the lads and myself were in the Richmond Arms enjoying a pint when out of the blue, the peace was shattered by the sound of hailstones—but how could that be, it was a beautiful late summer's night. On going outside we were amazed to see the whole town ablaze, and the heavy bombs started to fall. Everyone—civilians—firemen—River Thames, Naval and Civil firefighters—took a hand in fighting the fires but when I had to leave at 4.30 in the morning the place was still on fire. It was reported that 36,000 incendiary bombs fell that night with 26 heavy bombs on Richmond Hill.

'One Sunday afternoon, with all the troops at a show at the Hammersmith Palais, Penge was terribly bombed and we were ordered out of the Palais, regardless of who we were, and had to help out. I've often thought how fortunate it was the bombers never hit the Palais. The place would be solid with all colours—creeds—nationalities of every fighting force. Another Sunday afternoon I even had a go at singing at the Palais when Gerry Wilmot was Compere. I've always been able to adapt myself to any situation but can you imagine trying to perform in front of a crowd like that, and all the while—cat-calls from your mates—sit down, you silly c———all this whilst the bombs whistled down.

'After the fire raid all the lads went out to help themselves and many a woman was dressed in the height of fashion with clothes taken from beautiful models which turned out to be dummies in blasted shop windows. One character even had what was thought to be a woman in a fur coat in the blacked out billet, but which turned out to be a tailor's dummy—what a laugh. Things had begun to get too hot, and after the fire of Richmond we had to move out to a secret destination—which turned out to be the Convent of the Sacred Heart at Roehampton.

'Nobody had made us aware of the fact that this place had received a terrible hiding—consequently when shown to our sleeping quarters there was many a shock—especially upstairs when one had to go to the toilet, only to find on opening the door—there was just a void on the other side. One bloke nearly lost his balance and just missed falling out. We soon established ourselves here, but the place was so eerie, particularly with everything burned out, but we soon had the convent cookhouse in working order and steam ovens controlled by a huge boiler in the yard.

'We were there as a holding company, kitting out incoming troops, and seeing them off to different theatres of war, and we had about 500 to feed. The system still prevailed—up at 4.30 in the morning—imagine it—half asleep, walking down strange unlit corridors, with statues standing in dark corners—suddenly an organ strikes up in the burnt out Church, and from nowhere a Black Robed Nun would glide by without a murmur, and I'd end up in the cookhouse in a cold sweat. At night some of the lads would remove statues from plinths and, wrapping themselves in sheets and standing on the plinths themselves, wait for the boys coming in the worse for drink—the statues would suddenly move—and "Panic Stations".

'Having access to certain rations not generally available obviously put cooks in a bargaining position in many fields. We ourselves were always well fed, as likewise were all of the Regimental Police, and there was never a shortage of the "other". In fact in one particular wing of the convent stood a row of single rooms allotted to the cooks due to the unearthly hours they had to be up. It came as no real surprise when one of the Caretaker Nuns registered a complaint about the goings-on in her Convent. But we were at a loss to know how she had found out about it until, on looking out of the windows, we found the trees festooned with Army-issue Durex. When we were lined up in front of an officer, I explained that as it was near Christmas, and having no balloons, we had substituted Durex to decorate the trees. The officer gave a look of genuine disbelief.

'About this time I was banished to Banstead where there was a "Dump", the reason for this being—we had had a dance in one of the undamaged halls and I had had a number of dances with Quarter Master Cowell's "lady" and he wasn't too suited. Next night I had to mix, bake and cool 1,300 Bread Buns whilst another Military Ball was taking place. I started mixing the dough, and it took all night to raise, cut, bake and hand over to the Mess Room orderly. Next day was a Gala day in aid of War Weapons with Military Bands and the public were invited to stalls, sideshows etc. Unbeknown to me the orderly had stacked all the fresh-baked Buns on top of each other whilst hot, and the result was they had set hard. QM Cowell took advantage of this, and set up a Stall with Bottles to knock down—and for balls to knock them down with—"3 of Private Smith's Buns a Penny". Didn't I take a verbal beating, not only from all the Boys but the local population as well.

'I packed my kit, and off to cook for a detachment of "Bantams" who worked on the Banstead Dump, but the cooking methods were easy on an ordinary gas stove, the rations coming daily from Roehampton, and none to spare. This place was far removed from the War, and deadly quiet, our entertainment being confined to Church Parties and a few pints in the Woolsack. About a month later I was sent back to the Convent and became Sergeants' Mess cook. I became a dab hand at pastry, filling pies with onions, Corn Dog and potatoes, and another speciality—Salmon and Pea pie, which was eventually taken on as a special dish. The idea was to create an impression, and salads were made to look like a picture—'too good to eat'. The best cuts of meat and rashers from the now "Sgt Cook", looking after his mates, and I had one helper in the kitchen and a dining room orderly, with no problems for cookng—gas ovens, hot water, electric potato peelers, everything, and when the opportunity arose I was barman in the Sgts Mess.

'I then became Officers' Mess cook—similar food, but I received amounts of cash to try and buy fresh greens or other things. I noticed a sloping wall which led down from the Officers' Mess kitchen to a dividing wall between the convent and land next door. Often the ducks from the Pond would roost near the wall at night, and you won't be surprised to learn that the ducks began to dwindle, and the officers were amazed at the fare, but never guessed how it was come by, until my orderly acquired some duck eggs, and, having boiled them, they were found to be ready for hatching—all was revealed, the orderly had obviously robbed a duck's nest and I was sent back to the cook-house.

'Then the General of the Army Catering Corps came and inspected us, and decreed that the cooking in future should be the field kitchen method, so back to Dutch ovens and Sawyer boilers, brick and clay fires, and fears for the future. These were soon realized when the orders came—Right, lads, pack up and get on parade—a dark winter night, 1942—Quick March—down to Barnes Station, on to the train, with windows blacked out, and away. All kinds of rumours, but it couldn't be abroad as we hadn't had embarkation leave—but sure enough, early next morning the train drew up alongside a huge ship in Victoria Docks, Liverpool.

'We were amazed to see would-be deserters handcuffed to the ships rail—later to be set free and told to swim for it if they wished, when we were well out to sea. The ship turned out to be the USS *Coamo,* and carried 200 passengers in peace time, but we had a complement of 1600, with meals on a Rota, and orders to sleep with our gear on. Once again we were away, and not long after we saw the biggest array of vessels ever set eyes on, lying up in the Kyles of Bute in Scotland. Ships of all types—Troopers—Battleships—Subs—you name them they were there. That night we were moving—a huge diamond convoy, flanked by the Royal Navy, and covered by Shackleton Aircraft.

'You can imagine the thoughts of everyone—is this the long awaited invasion—but I had heard a whisper, and was told to post my letter home in the navy box, and don't tell anyone but the invasion is on, only not in France—but in "North Africa". No wonder we were so long at sea, and up to the teeth with

American food—fags—coffee and coke. We could smell tea and woodbines wafting from the *Orsina* in the distance. Well—apart from some old tramps vanishing in the wake we finally arrived twenty-one days later at Algiers, and the confusion of landing in the Dark—bombs—bullets—ships sinking in the harbour—utter chaos—and in the midst of all this—Right, Ted—brew up.

'And so the methods of Huyton, Liverpool, came into play, alongside a huge store house—timber from anywhere, ration boxes, anything that could burn—and there we brewed up and heated hundreds of tins of McConachies—Rice—Bacon—Beans, any bloody thing, and dished them out right left and centre—What did you get?—just my bloody luck, Soya Sausages—Who likes this bloody fat bacon?—and all the time the crash of bombs—anti-aircraft shells—tracers—a thousand Guy Fawkes rolled into one. On top of this the need to obey the calls of nature—You men, dig a six foot deep trench twenty feet long, get cracking—and soon hundreds of blokes queueing up and in no time it was full, covered over and a fresh one dug. This was the method right through the Campaign, right to Tunis and back.

'Next day everyone up bug-eyed—drum up—tea, tea and more tea—and down to the docks. Here order was being attempted out of the previous night's confusion, and once again pouring rain, and more tea—Who the hell do they think we are, bloody fire-eaters?—but the tea was made and another ship, the *Quenlenna* I think, pulled alongside and the troops poured aboard. It seemed the whole British Army had got aboard and finally we set off in the pitch darkness and hugging the coast, and the sound of water lapping the plates. Jesus—what's going to happen here if we're torpedoed, the result was the deck was crowded before first light, and with self-preservation to the fore I and my mates managed a dixie of tea and some fresh bread from the matelots aft, and made the most of it.

'Suddenly the skipper's voice over the tannoy—"Attention, everybody, in the event of this ship being bombed or torpedoed it's every man for himself as there are no lifeboats." Then it happened—grown men going frantic—Oh Jesus, let me out—you filthy bastards—oh mother, and real remorse. It was at times like this that I advised my mates to keep well clear of the crowd, and if the worst came to the worst to get away fast.

'However, after a very fast passage we made Bone by nightfall, and this time the welcome was worse than ever, with the sky ablaze and bombs falling thick and fast, and we were away into a Tabacoup. It reminded me of Hammersmith Palais—literally thousands of troops lying anywhere, and when the drones of the planes faded away someone started a sing-song which was soon picked up and carried on late into the night.

'Next morning—midst lots of drumming up—most of the lads had gone, and we heard that the Hampshire Regt had been literally obliterated within eleven days of landing. We had lost some on landing and it was terrible to see the graves that had been opened, and the blankets wrapping the bodies had been stolen. Grave-robbing was rife all through the Desert Campaign, so I believe, and it was generally accepted that the Arabs were the culprits.

'More days and nights of bombing and once again get loaded up and away, always east. It was at this time we met a much battered American column coming out of the line, and we exchanged condolences. An officer told a group of us, Man—your boys sure are hot stuff with them there mortars. They can hit a dime at a mile, and give nine cents change—and off we went to a village called Maurice. As soon as we unloaded, all the Arabs in the neighbourhood came out, and the lads wasted no time setting up shop, and bartering for holed socks, vests, anything of no value. In return we got clocks, watches and other accoutrements, which we had to throw away as soon as we moved forward on officers' orders.

'At Maurice I made a real friend with the local Boulangiere, M. Tisserand, and his family. We found we had a lot in common. His oven was a primitive affair like a huge dutch oven, heated by brush wood which was delivered by an Arab every day in exchange for French Bread. At this particular time I was entirely on my own and seldom saw an Officer or Sgt, and I had a free hand more or less. I was beginning to "Parle la langue beaucoup" and the Tisserand family made me their own and I came and went as I pleased. On Christmas Eve they invited me to Supper with a mate of mine, a soldier in the signals, and I have never been to such a feast before or since.

'Around the table were M. Tisserand and Mme. Tisserand, their four children one of whom was Marie Elaine about six years old, an old lady who I took to be the Gran, and some other people who must have been French settlers and received us young soldiers well, obviously hating the Hun and making no bones of it. As guest of honour I had to do the carving, Viand de Boeuf, Goose and a Turkey that had somehow roamed the only street in Maurice and survived my pot. There was beautiful soup (macaroni), Pomme de Terre, artichokes, dates and nuts, with wine at every touch and turn, even snails if you wanted them, and on top of all this a beautiful Christmas Cake baked in that primitive oven. I sang "Silent Night" and they all joined in.

'In my search for fuel in Maurice I nearly had to burn the place down—trees—fences—doors—tables—chairs—the lot. One morning I evolved a system of achieving quick results in cooking in one of the barns, making a twelve foot trench of rows of biscuit tins full of fresh water, with timber laid in the gaps between the rows and saturated with high octane petrol. We then laid more tins filled with canned bacon, beans and soya sausages, and topped up with water. Then a big canvas flap over the barn door—one rifle shot in the timber—and BOOM, a flash like a bomb going off, and in no time hundreds of troops plied with breakfast and tea, and the whole village awake shouting "Allemange Bomba", dogs barking and utter confusion.

'I really believe the only reason we were moved on was the attention the night bombers started to give us, and the fact that I had burned the place down in the quest for fuel and there was no accommodation left. But we were sorry to leave—and how those kids cried when we moved out. Some days later we found ourselves in a Military Barracks in a beautiful fishing village called La Calle on the Barbary Coast I believe. This was like a lagoon, and the fish could be seen clearly from the quay-side on the silver sand, an ideal place for swimming too.

'It was here we came across two American soldiers manning a machine-gun, apparently forgotten about when the Army moved on, and glad to have someone to talk to. They told us they owed each other millions of francs playing poker. They were so bored and one said to me, "Boy, those Cooks Tours are a load of seditious propaganda", and we soon found out why. Everything we have in England like beetles—ants etc., are 10 times larger, and even the flies are ravenous too.

'Then came the order—get loaded, and ever eastwards. When we set off the weather was great, with tropical kit the order of the day, but we're going higher, up the Tebousouk Mountains, and by the time we reached the top we had every stitch of clothing on, even our greatcoats. So much for Africa, but now the hastily-made grave-yards were becoming more evident—Swastikas—Stars and Stripes—Union Jacks, and many other crosses everywhere, but the notices say—Keep moving—Keep your distance, until the following morning we awoke to find ourselves in amongst a grove of trees on a farm high on the plateau of Tunis.

'At this time we had become detached from the main body and joined another group parked in the grove. We removed the frame and canopy from the back of the lorry and used this as a tent. I made the acquaintance of a lad who had been a butcher's assistant in Liverpool and soon we had rigged up our field kitchen—but what to eat? There was livestock all over the place and any amount of Guinea Fowl, and here we were with only our "corned dog". During the night the cry went up, "Snake, Snake", and under the confusion much banging and squawking. Needless to say every one had roast fowl next morning and milk which we bartered from the Arabs who tended the cattle, eggs were plentiful, and we were on to a good thing, we thought until on leaving the place the Arabs waved us off, and we later found blankets, boots, personal belongings missing—we the robbers had been robbed.

'We now found ourselves surrounded—but it was only the First, Eighth and French Armies joining for the Victory March into Tunis. What a sight—four huge columns stretching for miles, and the whole German Army surrendering along with the Italians and whoever were our enemies. Flowers—Roses—happy wisecracks—"Get yer knees brown" from the Desert Rats—and next stop Le Bardo, about a mile from Tunis, with the taking over of the enemy stores and captured equipment. Here I made many more friends, French families who had escaped in the fall of France, the Raymondies from Metz, the Deveraux's from Lille, and many more whose one thought was to get back home. There was also a young German Tank Sergeant who was a prisoner, and pleaded with me to see his family in Potsdam when we got there—his name clearly imprinted in my mind, Wolfgang Wenzel, of Africa Corps Tank Regiment, who lived at 23 Groshevan Strasse, Bablesburg—and terrified at the prospect of being interned in Canada. I often wonder where they all are now.

'It was sweltering weather, we wore only shorts, stocking tops and boots, and were all bleached blonde. The Officer at Le Bardo had made one of the lads dig a trench for a toilet about two feet wide and ten foot long, and this lad literally got dug in—we forgot about him until grub up and when I looked over towards the trench there was no sign of him. Thinking he'd gone into the Tent we never bothered, and it wasn't till late in the afternoon we found he'd got so deep he couldn't get out and had collapsed with the heat.

'A cause of laughter that happened often was the number of blokes who fell backwards into the toilet. When crossed timbers had been fixed at each end of a trench and a pole put along as a seat, with a tarpaulin around as a screen, the new toilet was declared open and the old one filled in. We had a chap who chased a jack-rabbit across what was rated as a field, near Bizerta, and he almost disappeared in what was thought to be a bog. His shouts were terrifying as he thought he was sinking, and when they went to pull him out, it was soon realised he'd fallen into a toilet pit. Later we found Italians had billeted in that field—on reflection North Africa must be one of the richest growing soils in the world.

'It was on 15 May 1943 that I ate some German dehydrated Sauerkraut and collapsed an hour later with vomiting and belly-ache. I was rushed to 1st Casualty Clearing Station in Tunis and whilst there two organised Raids on the Casbah routed out numbers of German and Italian troops who had gone into hiding there. I was returned to Active Service on 18 June, and once again the order came—Get loaded, and I said Goodbye to No. 5 Beach Ordnance Detachment and with hundreds of troops boarded cattle wagons at Douanne railway station. Where to this time?

'Tea was brewed from the Steam-engine and toilet necessities made from the running board of the moving train, much to the amusement of the Arabs, but we were past caring and three days of rough riding brought us to a station on the Tunisia–Algeria border. A crowd of youngsters were drilling with precision, and we, having drummed up and made a mess of rice and powdered milk, were so absorbed in this, also the need to stretch our legs after the long ride in the cattle trucks, that we never saw what was going on at the other side of the track. The whistle blew—everyone aboard—and too late, we had been robbed of everything—boots, coats, blankets, the lot, and so back to Bone.

'We were billeted at the Cafe Continental, and whilst there two of those supposedly mysterious Bedouin women made a play for the Sergeant and myself. On taking off their Robes and Yashmaks, we were amazed to see they were beautiful with modern European clothes on. On taking them back to the Casbah, they put on their Robes and we went to their flat. One of these girls was married, and a photo of her husband on the wall, in uniform, I think he was in that Berba company—anyway other Arabs came in, and one hell of a row blew up, so we got out fast and ran like hell out of the Casbah, with dogs—Arabs—kids, everyone shouting and pointing at us. A French song was popular here—"Aprés la Guerre fini—Soldat Anglais Partee—Madamoiselle Beaucoup Piccaninny—Aprés la Guerre Fini".

'I paid a visit to Maurice to say farewell to M. Tisserand, then off again in open trucks—all through the night—freezing cold, to a seaport called Philipville. Once again, Drum up, burn anything for fuel, and Quick march down the coast road. Excitement began to overtake us as we came alongside the passenger ships at the Quayside, but we were marched on and, on entering a gap in the sand dunes, I was amazed to see a valley full of tents, Marquees, and thousands of troops of all nationalities camped there.

'It turned out later that we were all bound for home and the invasion, but meanwhile the Provost Sergeants were picking out recruits for Italy and India, but I was sent to an Allied Officers' Mess. We sailed for home shortly after the American Thanksgiving Day on board the *Duchess of Bedford,* inside left in the convoy to the *Monarch of Bermuda.* Beautiful sunshine—deck races—cinema shows, the lot. Then two days out of Gib with the convoy heading west—seven minutes to Port and seven minutes to Starboard—I was sitting on the fore deck when the two distress signals go up, and next thing—panic stations—the *Monarch of Bermuda* is on top of us—life boats slung outboard are cracked up in between the two ships—everyone on both ships rushes on deck—and the *Duchess,* with a 45 degrees list, crunches into the *Monarch* amidships from the waterline to the superstructure and rips her open.

'Bells are ringing—sirens wailing—Is this it, after all we've done—but eventually the ack ack ship comes over, and orders the *Monarch* about and away they go with much blasphemy aimed at us on the *Duchess* for carrying on to port, when the rest of the convoy is steering starboard. We put in at Gib for a quick repair, and then, our bows stove in, we left the convoy at full speed for home. We arrived, on 28 November, at the very place in Liverpool from which we had left, but this time to a tumultuous welcome, with bands playing and crowds of people dancing. Then on to a train down to the Cheddar Gorge for regrouping before going home for Christmas 1943.

'From Cheddar Gorge to Wellington Barracks, Dorchester, but the Yanks moved in and we moved out to Weymouth. During the training for the invasion which was taking place from Portland Bill, with landings at Weymouth Beach, the E boats came in close, and I witnessed the Yanks being literally cut to ribbons, as they didn't have a pea shooter between them, and the survivors swimming ashore.

'But for me it was Goodbye to the lads. It seems my health had started to deteriorate from the time of eating that captured German food. I was 39 days in Weymouth Hospital, 15 days in Banstead Hospital, 21 days in Kingston Convalescent Depot, then to St Omer Barracks, Aldershot. Doodle bugs were on the go, but in the Autumn I was off to Aberystwyth and eventual discharge on 28 December 1944. And so back to Civvy Street, with three red Service Chevrons, the Africa Star and some snapshots to show for it all.

'I never exploited my cooking ability, but often wish I had. I've had many jobs, all associated with Rigging and Erecting, and have been in charge many times, but always had the urge to move on, though not from Teesside. My wife and I have seen four of our five children off from home, and fortunately none has been involved in war, and cannot believe half the things we tell them of what went on in those days. Perhaps it's just as well, as, though it seems to be an adventurous war, I must admit I had it good, and though we had some trying times, there were others who had it far worse. Come to think of it—I often wonder who dealt the cards of life. It gives one lots of food for thought.'

5 *Stalag III D—Berlin*

'Prisoner of War! It did not seem possible. The sun was bright and the sky cloudless. A perfect day on a Mediterranean island. But the grim reality was there. German soldiers with tommy guns and rifles walked in our midst. We were being herded like cattle.'

For Lance-Corporal Norman Norris, aged twenty-one, capture in Crete that glorious June day in 1941 was the start of four years' herding and goading by the Germans. For most of the time he was in Stalag III D, Berlin, where British prisoners of war were forced to work on the laying and repairing of railway tracks and other menial tasks helpful to the German war effort. Though acts of sabotage were carried out wherever possible, it was a humiliating as well as arduous existence that made revenge the sweeter.

The 40,000-word journal Norris wrote while those degrading years were still fresh in his mind gives a rare close-up of how retribution came home to the Germans. After the brutalities he had seen and experienced, he shows an understandable relish in the closing scenes of the war—the mass air raids on Berlin, the crumbling morale of German soldiers and civilians alike, the crushing defeat and ruthless occupation by the Russians they so feared.

Norris, a Londoner from Peckham, had joined the Royal Army Ordnance Corps just a year before his capture. He was sent to Egypt in November 1940 and had served in the campaign in Greece before coming to Crete. For days before the end came, he and his friend Jim had been caught up in a chaotic retreat from Suda Bay to Sphokia under constant strafing from the German bombers and fighters that dominated the sky. Like hundreds of their fellow-prisoners they were already exhausted when German bayonets pointed them back the way they had just come—that nightmare route over the mountains to Suda Bay.

'Piles of equipment lay everywhere, stacks of rifles with their butts smashed. Already a long line of men were making their way to the top of the cliffs overlooking Sphokia, but this time the column was moving much slower than it had on the journey from Suda. Nobody had eaten well for days. The Germans promised food at the first halt. That was sufficient to get us moving.

'We found ourselves once again on the cliff top and looking out to sea across the many miles of water that separated us from Egypt and all our dreams of good food and leave in Alexandria. Just as we began to march a German soldier singled out a British soldier next to me in line and told him to carry part of his mortar equipment. Had it been me at this stage I would have sunk to the ground under such a weight. Only the promise of food led us on, but towards the end of the day it became apparent that we would not be getting any.

'A large number of us were herded into a field which was surrounded by a dry stone wall, and as we entered each man was roughly searched for concealed weapons. Told, with another promise of food, that the march would be resumed at daybreak, everyone sank to the ground. Drinking a little of the supply of water we still possessed, Jim and I pulled the blanket we shared over the top of us and tried to sleep. I awoke when Jim nudged my elbow and said, "How about us getting away, anything would be better than this."

'Remembering that my father, who had been a POW in the First War, had received the biggest thrashing of his life for a three-day escape, I looked at the patrolling Germans with apprehension.

' "If we could get to the hills we shall probably find food and shelter in a remote village," Jim said.

'The burly Scot talked me into it. We were already lying against the wall surrounding the field and, folding our blanket, waited for the next patrol to pass, slid over the rough stone and made our way on hands and knees across the adjoining fields. So far so good, but to make any real headway quickly we decided to get on to the road. This was our mistake. We thought we had considerably lengthened the distance between ourselves and our captors, when we rounded a sharp turn and heard an order barked out as if to waken the dead: HALTEN! We had walked right into a German road block.

'Two Germans came forward with flash lamps and rifle muzzles pushed into our stomachs. They spoke English and we told them that we had decided to walk back to Suda during the night as it was cooler. They smiled at this, then one pointed to a big heap of stones by the road and said "You will sleep there". One of them pointed to the mountains and then tapped his rifle butt, saying "Get away and you will be shot". We dozed on our pile of stones till daybreak.

'We woke to see six German Paratroopers sitting by the road block, eating bread and sausage in the morning sunshine. Looking at us they smiled. We looked back, not at their faces, but at the bread and sausage they were chewing. The hint we gave them with our eyes had no effect. The bastards gave us nothing. Soon we heard the sound of marching feet and into view came a long line of POWs herded along with an escort of German Paratroopers on either side. After a short explanation from our German hosts for the night we were handed over.

'Some of the men we now found ourselves amongst were in a pitiable state, walking with rags wrapped round their feet, shoulders hunched, beards prominent. Food was still promised, but never materialised. We passed a German seated by some boxes at the roadside, quite drunk, his head in his hand, with an open tin on top of the boxes. I snatched this to find it about one third full of marmalade with about a dozen wasps buzzing around inside. Getting rid of the wasps, Jim and I shared the contents. One halt was by a field of wheat and Jim and I set to husking the ears between our hands. When we had about a third of a dixie full, we poured enough water to cover the grain and boiled it over a fire. After ten minutes of boiling, the corn was a hard as ever.

'At intervals the stench of death became almost overpowering. Some bodies had been hastily buried but only under a thin covering of earth. Others lay unburied, their faces unrecognisable. We saw two blackened bodies lying with a smashed Bren gun, even the uniforms unrecognisable, but obviously two British or Commonwealth soldiers sacrificed in the rearguard. Just as well their sightless eyes could not see us marching into captivity.

'About mid-day we received our first issue of food whilst in German control—a packet of British army biscuits and a tin of bully between two men, and once more set off. The men now to be pitied were those whose boots were falling to pieces and who were just hobbling along over the sharp stones cutting their feet into a bloody mess. We saw one man ahead fall from the line of marching men and roll into the ditch. Jim and I recognised the face staring skywards. Getting into the ditch we attempted to get him to his feet but he just moaned for us to leave him there to die. His boots had fallen to pieces on the march. Both feet were bloody and lacerated beyond description. Stepping into the road, I waved to a passing German motor-cyclist. Luck was with us. He allowed us to put him in the empty sidecar and drove off in a cloud of dust toward Suda.

'Passing through a Cretan village towards evening, we managed to get a huge piece of goat's milk cheese from a wizened old man in exchange for our few remaining drachmas. But within a short time we were desperately hungry again. The evening drew on. It began to get cold after the intense heat of the day and once more we lay down to sleep in the open.

'Next morning the Germans began to force-march us along. They could afford to do this as fresh German guards were brought along frequently. Dysentery now began to take its toll. Men faltered in their step and everyone was utterly worn out with the agony of placing cut and blistered feet on the sharp stones. Faces were drawn, shoulders drooped, sheer will power kept them going.

'It now became apparent that our next meal would be at the end of the march. We passed slowly through another Cretan village where Jim and I had a piece of luck. A Cretan farmer gave us a piece of raw goat flesh. Later on in the day we halted near a potato patch, scraped some out with our hands and prepared a meal. We found an aluminium box by the roadside, cut the meat up with an old razor blade, and, with the potatoes, cooked a kind of stew. The meat was extremely tough, but it certainly did revive us.

'All afternoon we were force-marched on the last leg of the journey. It seemed impossible to place one foot in front of the other. Men walked in a daze. Still we came to places where bodies lay mutilated and tried to hurry past the sickening stench of death. Towards the end of the afternoon Suda Bay once more came into view. Now men were almost dropping at the roadside. German troops being transported along the road stopped to photograph us. It seemed a great joke to them seeing us in such a condition.

'Marching down into Suda, we could see the terrific destruction wrought in the Bay, ships with their upper decks showing above the water and the far end of the Bay thick with oil and every part of the shore covered with the slimy black filth. Reaching Canea we found still more destruction. Shutters hung crazily from windows. Piles of rubble and desolation everywhere. The capital of Crete would not forget these German swine in a hurry.

'With dragging footsteps we finally came to a halt at the site of the 7th General Hospital. A long line of men were forming up for the promised food, and Jim and I joined the queue. After a while we were told it would be issued in the morning instead. Men sank wearily to the ground. Jim and I spread our blanket in a small depression and fell asleep exhausted.

'We both slept until the sun began to feel really warm on our bodies, then, ravenously hungry, made our way to a crowd of men who were being issued with food. After a long wait we again got a packet of army biscuits and a tin of bully between two. They vanished in a few mouthfuls. This was only the second issue of food in four days. At mid-day we got a small ladle of boiled rice with raisins added.

'This was our daily ration and hunger became so acute that men could think of nothing but food. A black market sprang up with the German troops, sums of money, watches, rings, anything of value were passed over for food. It was pitiful to see even wedding rings passed to the eager-eyed German swine in exchange for a few crusts of bread, or maybe a special bargain, a tin of British army food.

'As each day went by, men became weaker and weaker. One day a German officer promised food for those joining a working party, erecting tents. When the job was finished the officer gave an order and a soldier went into a tent and returned with a sack over his shoulder. The contents were tipped on to the ground in front of us: mouldy crusts of bread as hard as a brick. The Germans laughed as they watched us pick them up.

We soaked them in water and scraped off the green mould before eating them.'

For Norris these nightmare conditions were to continue until he reached the comparative comfort of a POW camp near Berlin that August. From Crete the prisoners were shipped to Salonika in an Italian cargo boat flying a swastika. With dysentery rampant, hundreds of men were packed into the stifling darkness of the hold, only allowed to the latrines on deck in 'extreme emergency'. Above them they could hear the Germans, drunk on Cretan wine, singing and shouting. They tauntingly sang down at them that popular British song, 'The Siegfried Line', and when the prisoners defiantly took it up, a German officer ordered the hold to be completely battened down.

On the quayside at Salonika an elderly German soldier speaking good English taunted them as they disembarked with such remarks as 'England has now lost the war' and 'You will now work for the German Reich'. They were housed in bug-ridden hutments, and lived mainly on hard tack biscuits boiled in water to a sloppy mess. The guards were trigger-happy. One English prisoner had washed his shirt and was hanging it on the wire to dry, when the German sentry without warning shot him in the stomach. 'Feelings ran high but we could do nothing,' writes Norris.

There was no medical aid at the camp for men now wasted away through lack of food and dysentery, and a particular nightmare was the train journey they eventually made from Salonika to Belgrade, two days and nights packed together in railway waggons, stifling by day, freezing by night. When they eventually arrived at Stalag III D 401, a prison-like factory at Neukoln on the outskirts of Berlin, they were immediately formed into working parties for jobs throughout the factory. Norris was detailed with some other men to break up old lorry back axles for salvage. Weakened by lack of food, the strenuous work soon put him on the sick list and he was admitted to a hospital.

Even here, on his first night, he was made aware of his servile status under the Master Race.

'I entered the allocated ward to find all the patients were French prisoners of war, haggard beyond description, their bodies wasted away. As soon as I had settled down in bed, along the corridor came the sound of marching feet, the ward door was thrown open and in strode a German officer followed by at least six of his staff. As soon as he entered one of the Frenchmen shouted out an order which at first I did not understand, but looking round the ward I saw every man lying to attention in bed. Later I found out that the senior man in each ward brought the men to attention as soon as the German officer entered each ward.'

Norris spent nearly three months in the hospital before being pronounced fit to return to the camp. From then on he and his fellow-prisoners were kept busy labouring at the behest of their captors. Jobs during that freezing winter included loading scrap metal into trucks, building an air raid shelter, once unloading coke into the boiler room at the Ministry of Propaganda in Berlin. ('Ironical to say the least that British POWs should be helping to keep Goebbels' propaganda machine warm.')

On occasion Norris had glimpses of actual slave labourers—young Polish girls with rags wrapped round their bare feet digging drainage ditches, Jews in their striped clothing, and political prisoners, unloading railway trucks under the eyes of SS guards. One day Norris was sent to a factory to help load a lorry with old car batteries.

'The Germans had Jewish men in what looked like home-spun cloth suits emptying the acid from each battery into huge glass containers, and over to one side of the factory yard were a number of furnaces where the lead from the batteries was being reclaimed. The Jews employed on this job wore no masks for protection and coughed continuously, their lungs were being slowly eaten away. It was pitiful to see the pleading look in their eyes, but of course we could do nothing, death could only be their ultimate end.'

The POWs did what they could to make their labours as unproductive as possible.

'Often our camp Kommandant would have us on parade to tell us what he thought of us. He would remark as he walked along our ranks that understanding the German language seemed to be our great difficulty. We always seemed to understand *Essen* (food), *Schlafen* (sleeping) and *Fussball* (football), but we never understood *Arbeit* (work), which was all very true. We always replied 'Nicht Verstehen' to anything we regarded as unpleasant.'

When early in 1943 they were moved to another camp, at Zernsdorf, most of their time was spent relaying the railway track in and around Berlin and active sabotage became possible.

'On most railway engines was painted '*Rader mussen rollen fur den Sieg* (The Wheels must roll for victory). But often a train would be brought to a halt with one of the truck's axle lubricating boxes alight where some unknown prisoner had lifted up the oil box flap and inserted a handful of sand. This seemed to work wonders on overheating the bearing till in the end it burst into flames. One day we even saw the connecting link of an engine's driving wheels come adrift. This made a horrible mess and cries of sabotage rent the air.'

It was at the end of January 1943, with the news that Stalingrad had fallen to the Russian troops that the British POWs first began to see an undermining of the Berliners' smug belief in the inevitability of victory.

'The news was like a knife thrust into the heart of the German nation. The propaganda that "Stalingrad will be ours" came to a halt, and the daily papers were edged in black. All this, of course, raised our morale tremendously. Working in the railway sidings at Koenigswursterhausen we saw the all-white camouflaged trains coming through daily packed with German wounded from the Russian front. The fresh reinforcements being sent were not looking so confident now. The waggons in which they were travelling to the front had deep layers of straw on the floor to keep out the intense cold, but they were lacking in good warm clothing to fight in such extreme temperatures. The Russians on the other hand were excellently equipped.

'Berlin now began to experience air raids which grew in intensity as the months went by. At first our German guards and civilian engineers used to mock us, saying that the defence of Berlin was so great that all our planes would be shot down. Now, on one of our many trips through Berlin, we noticed that a gigantic camouflage scheme had been undertaken. From the Brandenburg Gate down through the Tiergarten the road was completely roofed over with steel wire netting to which were attached pine branches and green cloth to make the road blend into the grass and trees on either side of it. A complete lake had been covered in the same way. The Berlin underground railway, being so shallow, was dangerous to use as a shelter, and each entrance had a notice to this effect.

'In one of the open squares off the Unter den Linden, a so-called authentic Russian village had been constructed, complete with many captured Russian weapons. A huge banner was strung across the entrance to the "village", with BOLSCHEWISMUS CHAOS in large red lettering. Unfortunately for the Germans all this area was soon to become an even greater "NATIONAL SOCIALIST CHAOS".'

One day bombs fell near the camp.

'It was a beautiful day and the sky in one direction seemed covered with vapour trails. The air was throbbing, it seemed the very ground was shaking with the noise of the aircraft engines above. Suddenly the whine of bombs could be heard and we dived for shelter. The ground shook with the explosions and the camp was covered in dust. When it settled the camp was found unharmed but all lighting and water supplies had been cut and some nearby houses damaged. Later that evening members of the local population came to the camp to vent their anger on us. One man shook the wire shouting, in perfect English, "English bastards" and "English gangsters". I hope he understood the replies he got.

'Unfortunately for us, the bombing was giving us extra work. Apart from laying track, we now had to repair damaged sections and sometimes a shovel would clang against an unexploded bomb. At this time we had to take our picks and shovels back to camp each night so that we could be called out to any area. Marching out of camp at 6.30 am one morning with our picks and shovels on our shoulders, somebody started singing the Walt Disney dwarfs' "Hi-Ho-Hi-Ho and off to work we go". Within a second everybody had taken up the tune. Some were walking along nearly on their knees characterising the dwarfs in the film, and what with the laughing and singing and the picks and shovels banging together, the noise was terrific. That evening complaints began to come in from the local population about the unholy row so early in the morning and our camp Kommandant rebuked us in no uncertain manner. Suggestions from us that we should start work much later in the day brought no results.

'One local civilian was always making complaints about us. He owned a large timber yard just up the road from the camp, and as we marched daily to the station would make disparaging remarks about our parentage, which we returned. We had our own back on him later on—incendiaries from an American bomber burnt his timber yard to the ground.

'One day a number of us were detailed to go to Charlottenburg to load a lorry with timber. Just as we arrived the air raid siren went and looking up we saw the vapour trails of hundreds of planes and the German defence putting up all it could. In those American 1,000-bomber daylight raids they flew across the city dropping "carpets" of bombs that smothered everything within the area. Our German guards were just as anxious to get to the nearest shelter as we. In front of it stood a German policeman. On finding out from the guards that we were British prisoners of war, he refused us entry.

'By now parts of Berlin were well and truly burning. Our guards asked the policeman where we could shelter and he told them of a place some way down the road. This shelter was constructed with concrete rings buried in the ground and inside were sitting many young girls. They were Russians brought to Germany to work. The German woman in charge of them had a face hard as granite and when she found we were British gave us a look to kill. Many of the girls were crying. We sat through the raid trying to put on a bold front, while the ground shook as if an earthquake was trying to engulf the city.

'When we emerged after the all clear we saw unbelievable destruction. Fires were getting out of control, whole areas were obliterated in black smoke, past the Brandenburg gate large buildings were now heaps of rubble. That night with Berlin still aglow the RAF came over and dropped a very heavy tonnage of bombs to keep things disorganised. With the Americans bombing by day and the RAF by night, the Germans were at last understanding what war was all about. To try and pacify the Berliners, extra rations of cigarettes and Schnappes were issued. Not much consolation when a "blockbuster" has fallen.

'Unfortunately all these raids were not achieved without losses to the Allied airmen. Numbers whose planes had been crippled were now floating down on their parachutes into their own target area. One day we saw a crippled bomber crash out of sight not far away. Later I was walking to a railway shed for something when a voice called out from a clump of bushes: "Some raid eh, Bud!" Standing there was a man in his twenties wearing a sports coat and flannels and carrying under his arm a thin leather case with a zip fastener round. There not being any guards around I stepped into the bushes, whereupon the stranger said, "That will give the bastards something to think about."

His American accent was unmistakeable. I was so taken aback I said nothing.

' "Have a cigarette," he said, and from his pocket drew out a packet of Camel cigarettes! Whereupon he said he must be going and, after I had taken a cigarette, still struck dumb, he disappeared into the trees beyond. Stepping back on to the railway track, I saw a guard hurrying towards me. He had seen me walk out from the trees and immediately questioned me as to what I was doing and who I had been speaking to. Thinking quickly I explained that a German civilian had asked me for a match. He said in effect that that was a likely story as it was "Verboten" for German civilians to speak to prisoners of war and took down the POW number on my tag.

'That evening, by which time I had destroyed the Camel cigarette, I was taken to the Kommandant who demanded to know who the person was I had been speaking to. I told him I had never seen him before (true) and that it was simply a German who asked me for a match. After a little while he dismissed me, but told the guard to keep a close eye on me at work. To this day that stranger remains a mystery. I like to think he really was an American airman and that he succeeded in getting back home unharmed.

'Each night as the raids grew in intensity our Kommandant allowed our huts to be unlocked so that we could go into the air raid shelter we had been allowed to construct at the end of the compound. To make doubly sure we could get out in a hurry, in my room we had sawed through the iron grille supports over the windows until just a fraction of the metal remained, using a hacksaw we had acquired at work. And we had worked out a drill whereby two men on either side of the table would use it as a battering ram to smash the grille and windows in an emergency. Being roasted alive by our own incendiaries was not a happy thought.'

Norris had been able to make a primitive wireless set after obtaining a small crystal set, in exchange for cigarettes, from a German guard who had been a radio mechanic in civilian life. It was a notable event when the drum beats of the BBC overseas news service were first picked up and they were now able to surreptitiously listen in to news of Allied victories. The biggest boost to morale hitherto had been the arrival of Red Cross parcels. 'How those parcels changed us,' Norris writes about the occasion when they had first been delivered. 'Men who were morose and ill-tempered became almost completely changed, smiles began to appear where formerly was an empty vague look, good friendships sprang up. Men delighted in lighting their cigarettes in front of the German guards, who were strictly rationed. To eat a bar of chocolate in a German's presence really made them wince. They sometimes retaliated by breaking chocolates and soap into little pieces before handing them over and puncturing tins.'

It was with the arrival of a new Kommandant that an episode unique in Norris' experience took place.

'It was noticed that one of our men was making visits to this Kommandant in the evenings. This seemed strange. After all, what would the Kommandant want with a prisoner—surely not to talk about the weather! Along with others of us, our Sergeant Major thought it very suspicious. One evening he was sitting on the steps to his hut when the man passed on his way to the main gate. He told him not to go through the gates, whereupon the man turned on him and said, "Mind your own bleedin' business".

' "Go through those gates and I will be waiting for you when you come back," said the Sergeant Major.

'Taking no notice the man asked the sentry to open the gates and went through to the Kommandant's quarters. The whole camp now awaited his return. Eventually he came out from the Kommandant's office and stood waiting for the guard to open the gate. Within the compound on the other side stood the Sergeant Major. As the sentry opened the gate the man didn't have time to walk through. The Sergeant Major dragged him through and then proceeded to thrash him in front of the German guard. When he fell to the ground he was only picked up again for more punishment. He attempted to defend himself but it was hopeless against this Military Police Sergeant Major.

'Watching the beating for a moment the guard went and brought the Kommandant who came through the gate with his Luger drawn. He demanded an explanation. The Sergeant Major, who had seen service on the Rhine after the First War, pointed out that the outside of the barbed wire was for the Germans and the inside of the wire for the British prisoners and what he had just done he would repeat on anyone who had secret sessions with the Germans. The Kommandant replaced his Luger and marched back to his quarters.

'The man was a bloody mess and, though other men now wanted to continue the beating, the Sergeant Major sent him to his bunk. Never again did he have secret talks with the Kommandant. This was the only incident of its kind we had happen the whole time that we were in Germany.'

By the spring of 1945 it was evident, even to the most arrogant of their captors, that the writing was on the wall.

'Huge areas of Berlin were now heaps of rubble. On a trip to Spandau our lorry seemed to motor past endless shells of buildings. Roads which had once contained proud houses now looked like battlefields. Coming to a detour we saw where bombs had penetrated to the underground railway. A train had been caught in the explosion. It looked as if a gigantic tin opener had ripped the section open. We passed an ack-ack site. The twisted steel of the guns and the bomb craters that linked up with each other showed the tonnage that was being dropped. Faces in the street looked haggard. Lack of sleep, plus the news of the advancing Allied armies, had completed their disillusionment. Yes, Berlin had changed since 1941 when we first saw it, untouched by war, smug under Reich Marshal Goering's boast that no enemy plane would ever reach the German capital.

'Huge tank traps were now being dug, one at Koenigswursterhausen by Polish Jews, the last of many who had been marched from Poland constructing defences as the German army fell back towards Berlin. Those that had been unable to continue working during the march had been shot as of no further use. They looked pleadingly at us. The look in their eyes, showing that they knew they would eventually be murdered, was unforgettable. All this could be plainly seen by any German civilian. The misery inflicted upon different nations could be seen everywhere, from young Polish and Russian girls to their own former ally, the Italians.

'Large numbers of round holes were being dug at different vantage points. These were to be used by German troops operating the "Panzerfaust", a rocket-propelled anti-tank grenade. Hitler youth appeared with rifles and military equipment. It seemed that even schoolboys were going to be used for the final stand.'

For Norris, himself in great pain from a blistered hand that had turned septic, and his fellow-POWs, the beginning of the end came on the night of 14 April 1945 when they were ordered to pack their personal belongings and any remaining Red Cross food they might have.

'We were paraded to march but, owing to the intense air activity, the Kommandant did not give the order until the early hours of the morning. As the gates were flung open for the last time for us to march through, numbers of local civilians, mostly women, were waiting, imploring us to take them with us. One woman flung her arms round George Hamlet's neck, kissing him and pleading to be allowed to go with him. However, not one offer was taken up and we marched away from the huts and the barbed wire. Even the camp guards marching with us were glad to be marching westwards. With the advancing Russian soldiers discovering the hell-like conditions their compatriots were being kept in, it was little wonder that it was into British or American hands they wished to fall.

'In the morning of 16 April we reached Potsdam. It had been

raided the night before and there was chaos everywhere, with numbers of German soldiers hopelessly drunk. But as we marched through all this destruction, tough SS troops were erecting barricades in a desperate attempt to stem the Russian advance. Terror and panic could be seen amongst the civilian population. Our guards spread rumours that the Russians would murder us as well as the Germans if they over-ran us. We were even told that the Western allies had joined the Germans in their fight against Bolshevism.

'That night in the open country we were locked in a huge barn patrolled by guards. Unreeling a length of wire which I carried in my overcoat pocket, I managed to get an aerial slung across the barn loft and we heard from the BBC news that the Western Allies and the Russians were still thrashing the Germans simultaneously. Next morning we found the Kommandant and some of the guards had gone in the night, presumably to get home as soon as possible, discarding their uniforms en route. The weather was foul, pouring rain soaked every man to the skin. Occasionally Russian fighters came over to strafe any vehicles bringing supplies and we had to dive for cover. German petrol tankers could be seen burnt out from earlier attacks.

'Striking off from the main road our remaining guards led us to a farm to rest. Trudging into the farmyard with the rain lashing down, we expected to get under shelter at least, but the farmer would not allow us even into an outhouse. Tired out, men sat hunched down against the walls of the buildings. I managed to find a plank of wood and with a brick under each end to raise it off the sodden ground, I lay down against the side of the barn. During the day some German troops appeared, but they were deserters trying to get home. The farmer gave them bottles of wine and in no time some were drunk and singing loudly.

'Moving on next day the rain had stopped but air activity was increasing. A huge convoy of troops and guns was making its way past us along the bomb-cratered road, when out of the sky appeared Russian fighter planes. Their machine guns were already spewing destruction along the convoy before the Germans realised what was happening. Throwing ourselves into the ditch alongside the road we lay still for the return run. The Germans had a multi-barrelled light ack-ack gun mounted on one of the lorries, and this now began to return the fire. With the tracers streaming towards them, the Russian fighters made off, satisfied with the damage they had inflicted on the convoy. Red tongues of flame reached high in the sky from burning lorries.

'After what seemed like endless marching we once more sheltered at a farm. Food now was practically non-existent. I was down to spooning a tin of cod liver oil and malt which had been saved from a food parcel. Many men were eating raw potatoes found in one of the barns. My arm was now useless, the hand stinking and swollen, and a second swelling under my armpit gave excruciating pain with every movement. Going into the farmhouse I obtained a basin of hot water from one of the womenfolk but immersing my hand brought only momentary relief.

'Heavy rainfall once again lashed our faces as we marched on. With a moan the man marching next to me collapsed in the mud and lay as if dead. Loosening the man's clothing, Cliff Kirkpatrick diagnosed the trouble as a fit. He brought the man round, who, finding he was lying down in the pouring rain, inquired "Wot the Bleedin' 'ell 'appened?" Getting shakily to his feet, he was helped along with a man either side of him.

'Eventually we reached a small village named Senzke, but there was something sinister about this place. It was packed with German troops, with a high proportion of officers. It appeared it was being used as a HQ and even our guards were not happy about remaining there so we marched on and rested under some trees. An hour later Russian aircraft came over to strafe the village and, without any opposition, dived backwards and forwards as if enjoying themselves. Our few remaining guards were just as perplexed as we where to go next, when we had a stroke of luck. A French prisoner of war appeared and, after a battle of languages, finally made us understand that if we followed him he would take us to a representative of the Red Cross.

'Within a short while we came to a magnificent country mansion with a number of cottages scattered about. It seemed to be a small community on its own, farming the land and rich in dairy produce. The house itself was luxurious. Huge chandeliers hung in the main hall and many animal heads adorned the walls. On the upper floor at the top of the stairs stood a huge stuffed gorilla. A Baroness lived here, with her daughter, and she gave us a cold reception. Later we found that the daughter's husband was an officer in the SS and was fighting on the eastern front.

'The Baroness allowed us to use the barn to sleep in, but told our guards that we could only have potatoes to eat. How we eyed the chickens running loose, the pigs in their styes, above all the cows standing ready to be milked in their immaculate stalls. Arrogant to the end, the Baroness must have known that it was only a matter of time when we would take all that we needed.

'The German farm overseer wore the traditional jack boots and attempted to carry out the Baroness's wishes, but with the gunfire of the advancing Russian troops getting nearer each day he was unsure of himself. Amongst the farm workers were a number of Polish men and women and two Russian prisoners of war. After a while we made contact with the Red Cross representative, who was using this place as his HQ. He was a Swiss national and seemed a furtive type. We eyed him with suspicion, he seemed much too concerned with the Baroness. However, he did issue us some Red Cross food and cigarettes, which helped save the situation, though we noted that the Baroness was also smoking fairly heavily.

'After a couple of days we woke to find that all our remaining guards had left in the night except one, who must have been at least sixty and just did not know what to do. In the end he sought our advice. Seeing that the old boy was getting on, and that he had given us no trouble in the past, the advice was unanimous. "Get rid of your uniform, dad, and bugger off home." Thanking us profusely, he disappeared across the fields.

'We were now in a rather tricky position, sandwiched between the Germans and the advancing Russians, and, with the gunfire getting nearer, looked around for more protection. Exploring the farm buildings we discovered a plant for extracting alcohol from potatoes. Underneath lay vaults which were strongly built of brick and we decided we would take our chance there. We discovered we had made a wise choice when in one corner we found chairs and bedding that the farm overseer had moved down for his family.

'As the Russians drew nearer, shells and mortars began to fall in and around the farm. German anti-tank gunners, dug in to resist the Russian armoured attacks, drew terrific fire. The two Russian prisoners of war, who had now joined us in the vaults, said they would contact the Russian advance troops when they arrived. Having them with us was a real stroke of luck.

'Gunfire, coupled with the heavy explosions of mortars, now became intense. The Russians were pouring heavy fire on the area. Long lines of German troops could be seen running across the fields, their boots and uniforms covered with mud, as they tried to escape the withering fire. Some came running through the farm itself, with hunted looks in their eyes as they struggled to run even faster through the sea of mud. Two Polish prisoners of war, who were watching the fighting from the yard, were killed by one exploding mortar shell, mutilated beyond all recognition. A Polish girl running across the yard received severe leg wounds and was carried down into the vaults, where Cliff Kirkpatrick gave all the help he could.

'Two British POWs attempting to get a better view were also hit. One had his face entirely skinned from a mortar blast. But the real tragedy, as far as we British were concerned, happened a little later. With the advance of Russian tanks on the outskirts of the farm a German anti-tank gun still continued to fire. The

Russians now poured a withering fire at this last remaining gun crew, completely eliminating them. Unfortunately our Sergeant Major with another man was sheltering in a house near the gun site. A heavy tank shell went right through the walls, decapitating them both. It was indeed a tragedy after four years of imprisonment to be killed within minutes of freedom.

'The ground now seemed to shake with the weight of advancing armour. Then at last we saw the first Russian tank lumber into the farmyard. Our two Russian prisoners of war ran across to it, shouting and waving their arms. We saw the tank commander emerge from the turret, jump down and engage them in conversation. Within a short time we were all shaking hands and hugging each other. As other tank crews arrived they too received the same treatment. And so, on 29 April 1945, we were free at last.

'To soften up the German opposition for a further advance, the Russians now employed a remarkable weapon, the "Katusha", or "Stalin Organ". This was a mobile rocket ramp which fired off amazing numbers of projectiles. They put a long line of them across the fields, wheel to wheel, and at the drop of a hand poured what seemed to be an endless rain of fire into the retreating Germans. While they were still retreating, we wrapped the bodies of our two dead comrades in sacks and, with heavy hearts, buried them in the private garden of the mansion.

'Now that the Russians had taken over, the Baroness took orders instead of giving them. We no longer had to be satisfied with just potatoes. Within a short time chickens were being boiled and pigs were being slaughtered. And for the first time in four years we had fresh milk in abundance. The farm overseer tried to protest, but was ordered to keep quiet. Jim and I decided to look over his house. As a good Nazi, he no doubt had luxuries to show for it. We were rooting round in his bedroom when we heard him clumping upstairs. Seeing us calmly going through the drawers in his dressing table, he bellowed at us to get out. Taking no notice, Jim went over to the sideboard and found it locked.

After a struggle to get it open, he turned to the German and asked for the key. "Schweinrei!" he spat at Jim. At that moment heavy footsteps sounded on the stairs.

'The door slowly opened and into the room strode a Russian soldier, standing at least six foot tall and with his fur hat looking enormous. On either hip he sported an outsize pistol. Seeing Jim and I he gave a smile, but the smile vanished when his gaze fixed on the German. He could speak a little German and we managed to explain that we wanted the sideboard open. Drawing one of his pistols he pointed it at the German's head. Never have I seen a key produced and drawers opened so quickly.

'Inside the sideboard we found a huge stock of cigarettes, cigars and pipe tobacco. He must have been a good Nazi considering how scarce these commodities were in Germany. By now his wife, hearing the commotion upstairs, had joined us. After removing the entire stock of tobacco, we began sharing it out with our Russian key producer. At first he refused to accept any, saying we had found it so it belonged to us, but we insisted on stuffing his pockets with part of the loot. As a parting gesture he said that, if the German had caused us any trouble, he would take him downstairs and shoot him. On hearing this both the German and his wife nearly collapsed with fright, but Jim and I declined our friend's offer and went downstairs with him, where we walked away to seek other treasure.

'It was not long after this that the cry "FIRE!" rang out. With almost incredible speed flames were racing through the Baroness's mansion. Hungry flames licked at the fine furniture and priceless relics and soon the whole house was burning fiercely. As the staircase collapsed the gorilla standing at the head of the stairs, like the Roman centurion at Pompeii, slowly toppled forward and plunged head first into the inferno below.

'How the fire had started was a mystery. Our guess was that the Baroness had destroyed the mansion rather than let it be taken over by the Russian forces. Within a short while nothing remained but the charred shell of a once magnificent building.

'We were now ordered to move back out of the area and once more began to march—this time back towards Berlin. That night we rested in a farmhouse near the main road. My arm was now in a frightening condition and it was impossible for me to remove my boots, but I managed to get a place on a spring bed and slept as usual fully clothed. In the early morning we were awakened by heavy mortar fire, some falling in the yard outside. On the main road outside a Russian soldier on horseback was shouting something we could not understand, but his arms signalled us to follow in the direction he was riding. Running and walking we eventually came to a town called Nauen, heavily defended with tanks and troops. A group of SS troops had entrenched themseves in a wood off the main road and had the Russian supply transport under fire. This did not last long. We saw a number of tanks move out from the town and Russian fighter planes could be seen diving. Later we saw many German corpses in the wood.

'Desperate now for medical aid, I found a huge building in the town which was being used as a hospital. A Russian sentry led me down a long corridor to a huge panelled door, knocked and opened it and signalled me to enter. The room itself was enormous, and to my surprise seated behind a desk was a Russian woman in uniform. As I walked towards her she rose and came round in front of the desk. Giving her a smart salute I pointed to my arm, whereupon she spoke in a flood of Russian as she removed the rags I had wrapped round it. The stench was appalling and the hand looked like a claw. She applied a dressing that seemed to ease the pain almost immediately, and signalled that I was to return for further treatment.

'The Russians now accommodated us in a hotel in the town which had been cleaned up by Russian army women. Our first meal was served in a large room with photographs of Stalin, Churchill and Roosevelt on the end wall, each decorated with its respective flag. That evening we were invited to a film show, and seated with many Russian soldiers saw spectacular scenes from the Relief of Sebastopol and the breaking of the siege of Leningrad.

'Now that we had a place to eat and sleep men just drifted around the town. How satisfying it was to sit and watch the Russians marching hundreds of German prisoners along. These Germans who had raped almost every country in Europe were now being herded along in the same manner they had done to others. The SS troops still looked defiant, but "For you the war is over" could now be said with relish to these political louts.

'Walking through the town Jim and I were stopped by a German woman in a very distressed state. Would we go to her house at once? It seemed that a Russian soldier had entered the house and was extremely attracted to her daughter. Would we go along to protect her? This was a tricky situation, but we decided not to go. How could anyone explain to any Russian soldier that what he was doing was wrong, when his mother, wife, sister, might well have been ravaged during the German occupation of Russia? War is a filthy business. This Russian soldier might well believe in "an eye for an eye". We left the woman and walked on.

'Each day notices were posted in the town describing articles for confiscation. At first all radio sets were handed in, the following day all bicycles. Some of us selected nice chrome bicycles as the Germans wheeled them to the handing-in depot and went for a tour round the town. The Russians advised that those of us whose boots were now worn out should pick a pair from the hundreds of marching feet that were going into captivity.

'It was just after a Russian male doctor had lanced my hand and told me I would have to get treatment in a Berlin hospital as soon as transport was available, that news came that the road to the Elbe was open and the Russians put trucks at our disposal to transport us to the American Forces. Aboard the trucks we clambered. I had a seat of honour next to the Russian driver who proceeded to eat an enormous tin of pork with his knife as he drove along at breakneck speed. The sides of the roads were packed with French and Dutch civilians now freed from their labour and streaming homewards.

'We were halted on the banks of the Elbe whilst the Russians contacted the American forces on the other side. Many Germans implored us to take them across into the American Zone, but a deaf ear was turned on every plea. With the order to cross, each Russian driver slowly and carefully drove across the pontoons which at that point were the only link between the two zones, and handed their very thankful cargo over to the Americans. We watched them turn about and slowly drive back across the pontoons, once more eastwards.

'Soon I was lying in the operating theatre of a casualty clearing station, with a kind American nurse asking about where I lived as she gave me an injection and told me to count to ten. I woke up in a bed with clean sheets and an American Red Cross officer asking if I was hungry. Within a short time there appeared a banquet. Chicken, white bread, plenty of butter. Chocolate and cigarettes. It all seemed like a dream.'

6 *Prisoners of the Japs*

'So life went on, but without milestones, every day was just another day, and for that reason just that much harder to live through because tomorrow would be the same as today . . . '

The deadening monotony of life in a prison camp, as much as the physical hardships and the brutal treatment, is the underlying theme of the following two accounts of their experiences in Japanese hands, by a soldier and a civilian. Captain L. J. T. Marsh was captured at Singapore in February 1942 : Mr T. E. Walter, a Forest Officer, was interned two months later in Batavia, Java. Both spent more than three years in captivity, and, though internees had privileges denied to service prisoners, their ordeals have much in common—not least the nightmare periods they spent working on 'death-railways'.

Apart from lack of food, their greatest deprivation was news from the outside world. Without letters from home, without newspapers or radio to let them know how the war was progressing, they existed in a limbo, and it was only by communal effort that hope was kept alive. Both experienced the pangs of near-starvation, the tragedy of witnessing emaciated, disease-ridden fellow-prisoners dying around them, the demoralising fear of being beaten up by sadistic guards. But that they and tens of thousands like them survived was not entirely due to physical stamina. The final test was to keep soul as well as body together.

Marsh's description of the soldier who died, not from wounds or sickness, but from sheer despair, is more horrifying in its implications than any new recital of Japanese atrocities.

Born in Forest Gate, London, in 1913, Leonard Marsh, a Post Office worker, had been commissioned in the 57th (Wessex) Anti-Aircraft Brigade of the Territorial Army in 1935 and was promoted captain when he was called up for full-time service in August 1939. He was posted to Malaya in January 1941 and, following the outbreak of the war against Japan on 7 December, served with a bofors battery during the retreat of the Allied forces down the Malayan peninsula. He was at Singapore when the garrison surrendered on 15 February 1942 and some 80,000 Allied servicemen went into captivity.

After the war Marsh wrote a long and detailed journal of his experiences. It is an objective, unemotional account that would largely disappoint anyone looking for a Chamber of Horrors gallery of Jap monsters. Marsh suggests that many POWs, on their return to England, felt that the 'brutality angle' had been overplayed in British propaganda. 'We resented this because it had caused our relatives to worry a bit more than they need have done. On the other hand there was a lot of brutality and our propaganda people had a job to do and were undoubtedly building up public opinion against the Japanese. Fortunately the end came quicker than anyone thought.'

Although Marsh himself suffered hardships comparable to some of those portrayed in 'The Bridge on the River Kwai', most famous of all semi-fictional dramas of a prison camp purgatory, his most lasting impressions of those harrowing years are on a spiritual rather than a physical plane. Most of all he has been haunted by the memory of that young soldier who died from despair. 'I was with him and saw it all,' he writes. 'It will forever remain in my mind more vividly than the many acts of heroism and bravery I saw during the war.'

It is this death that Marsh leads up to in the following condensation of the basic experiences of a POW that he elaborates on in his journal. His account begins with his capture after the fall of Singapore on 15 February 1942.

'After the preliminary turmoil we did not see a great deal of our captors and became in general terms a vast mass of humanity in one heap with a perimeter guard of Japanese. As one would expect, like attracted like, and small groups of men with kindred outlooks developed naturally. In every group it was automatically accepted that tribulations and blessings were shared. If someone was without footwear a second pair of boots or plimsolls were found from somewhere. A packet of cigarettes became one cigarette between five or six friends each evening to make the stock last as long as possible. I still remember the occasion when one of the five in my group quietly sold a treasured typewriter, sharing the very small proceeds amongst his friends.

'With most material things non-existent, and food daily becoming scarcer, the benefits of comradeship within each small circle became the thing of greatest value and the strongest sustaining force in our daily round, which in the early days of our captivity literally held no future. For this reason everyone made the strongest effort to keep this light of friendship burning bright and whilst the selfish and unscrupulous, few as they were, were gradually excluded into solitude, the little groups became welded into something strong and durable.

'During the day we were employed on domestic duties or were taken out of the camp under guard to chop trees for firewood. But every night, after a meagre meal of rice, each small group gathered quite instinctively to play bridge, to plan escape, or just to speculate and toss around the daily rumours of big events that were always circulating in a camp cut off from all outside contacts—no newspapers, no wireless, no mail. The ever present question was "when are we going to get out?" Military experts, spiritualists, pyramidologists, anyone who might give us hope, were sought out and their opinions carefully listened to and debated.

'So life went on, but without milestones, every day was just another day, and for that reason just that much harder to live through because tomorrow would be the same as today. Even when, to us, momentous events happened, they were generally to our disadvantage. The rations were to be reduced, a task had been imposed by our captors, or accommodation was to be worsened. One of the breaks in monotony was the occasional raid by the Kempe tai, or Japanese Gestapo, when, however clear one's conscience, you never knew what was going to happen. I knew of one poor lad who was whisked away because he had a jar labelled "Radio-Malt". When the Japanese realised this did not mean the possession of an illegal wireless set, they could not admit a mistake without a loss of face. The lad therefore had to undergo some punishment before he was returned to the fold.

'The monotonous round of our existence eventually changed, and, in accordance with precedent, it was for the worse rather than better. The Japanese suddenly announced that large parties were to be transported to Thailand where camps were better, food was plentiful and the climate healthier. This was received with a mixture of pleasure and distrust, as clearly it sounded too good to be true. Then rumour crept in and slowly swept away the gilding on the official announcement. The Japanese were going to build a railway to link Bangkok with Rangoon and we were to do the work.

'The day came when my name was on the list for the next party and by that time we all knew that we were not going to a holiday camp. Our little group, which had already suffered some losses, now disintegrated in a general reshuffle and I was loaded with twenty-seven other men into a small covered goods truck at Singapore station. We were in that truck for three days and nights, each day allowed only one bucket of cooked rice and one pail of water per truck, before being decanted into a rural area in Thailand, where we were told we were going to march by night until we reached the site we were to work on.

'Few of us were in a condition to walk any great distance. We were all affected by the low rations we had been getting, and many were suffering from diseases such as malaria, dysentery and beri-beri. We were told to carry what we could and leave the rest and set off in darkness along a made road, Japanese in front to lead the way and Japanese at the back to whip in the stragglers. We rested occasionally and as dawn broke reached a small native village. I slept with many others on a raised platform in the village temple at the feet of a large Buddha. In the late afternoon we were roused and fed and at dusk were on our way again.

'I don't think anyone in the party could have said where we were on the map to within 200 miles, and at this stage nobody cared. Some had remained behind, unable to move on despite pleas or brute force, and where their destiny took them I never knew. The rest of us were merely thankful that we were still marching on a well made road. At dawn next day we were halted and told this was it. We weren't anywhere at all, but all the same this was it and we spread ourselves out over waste ground at the side of the road and made the best of it. Apart from a few stunted bushes there was no shelter, no houses, no huts, no tents. Our captors clearly did not regard it as anything unusual.

'After a day or so a number of us were marched off and taken by rail towards the interior. We travelled in metal boxes pinned to bogies pulled by a diesel lorry converted to fit the rails. The line was pleasantly undulating (as the guide books say) and the scenery was relieved by many railway waggons that had toppled to the side of the track. After about twenty miles we reached the end of the line, disembarked and were marched off into the jungle. We were soon halted in a clearing and told we had to wait for nightfall. After a look at our surroundings, I decided I had got to lighten my load and managed to exchange a camp bed I was carrying for half a bucket of water from a local resident.

'After dark the march started and, although it still remains vividly in my mind, I could not describe it in any detail. A Jap led the way with a hurricane lamp and 200 of us followed. I was well up with the lamp but what happened behind I never knew. There must have been a track but to us we just plunged into darkness and the jungle. There was no light whatsoever apart from the wretched hurricane lamp bobbing about in front. Uphill and downhill we went, just stumbling into darkness with mud, rock and roots underfoot.

'Occasionally we halted and at each stage some gave up and slept where they lay. At dawn a mere twenty or so straggled into a clearing, where there were a few ragged tents and a supply of boiled water and cooked rice. We never bothered about shelter. It was enough in this wilderness to find food and water and sleep where we lay. Throughout the day stragglers came in, many arriving just in time to start off again.

'This programme continued for several nights—I never did keep count—and then one morning, on a bluff overlooking a large river, we were told we were there and that our first job was to make a camp. A few primitive tools appeared and we started to attack the jungle. When a reasonable clearing had been made the Japanese issued our tentage. My team was better off than most as we had a twelve foot square tarpaulin to shelter eighteen of us. We slept nine each side and head to toe on a flooring of thin bamboos. Next day we had all planned the many things we were going to do to make our shelter more presentable when we were given the very unpleasant news that all men would now work on the railway.

'Before daylight came, roughly half of us were paraded to be marched off through the jungle to the railway workings. One shift worked all day and the other shift worked all night and the task allotted to our camp was to make a cutting through the shoulder of a limestone hill. The cutting when finished was about eighty yards long and up to forty feet deep. Australian prisoners were working drills to bore holes. The Japanese placed dynamite charges in them and fired them and we cleared away the debris. It was a very clear cut task and there was only one rule and that was that you never stopped working apart from one meal break on each shift. Even when the shifts changed over there was no halt, you just took a pick or shovel from someone else and kept it in motion.

'When a shift returned to camp there were many necessary tasks to perform, food to be collected from the cookhouse, water to be brought from the river for washing, water to be obtained and boiled to augment the meagre cookhouse ration. This also meant gathering quite a lot of firewood. As had happened in our times of leisure, the small groups formed themselves by automatic selection once again and to each man of the group was allotted one of the communal tasks. Additional to this were camp tasks such as carrying rice in bulk from river boats, digging graves and latrines and a hundred and one other odd jobs.

'I fell into a group of five and we lived together, marched together, worked together and slept together and were forever in each other's company, twenty-four hours a day, seven days a week. I can never remember a cross word. Perhaps we never had time to disagree.

'One of our team was a young lad, unmarried, unsophisticated, and perhaps more of an idealist than any of us. He was with us in all we did, he did his share and more, and, with the rest of us, he became thinner and weaker each day with the hard work and meagre rations. We were all reaching an advanced stage of malnutrition but, apart from this, all of our little group remained fit and avoided the diseases of cholera, malaria and beri-beri that were all around us. And then one morning before light when we were all being roused, this young lad said with a frightening air of finality that he was not stirring. He wasn't ill, he wasn't hurt, he had just decided he had had enough.

'The other four of us pleaded with him to change his mind, telling him of what our captors would do to persuade him, but all to no avail and we had perforce to leave him to join our working party.

'About the middle of the day I was sent back to the camp on some special errand and on arrival enquired for our missing team mate only to be told he was dead. Had the Japanese killed him? No, was the answer, he had just died. I hastened to our medical officer, a prisoner like ourselves, and asked him, "What did he die of?" The doctor answered, "Nothing that is in my book. He just decided he didn't want to go on living."

'I walked away and realised how much the others of us clung to the memories of our jobs, our wives and our families and wondered whether it was the strength of one's memory that gave the will to fight, live and survive. I wondered just why this young lad, with all of life ahead, had voluntarily let the vital spark of life flicker and die. Had we failed him? Or was it the sudden realisation that there was no future other than a blind trust he could no longer accept?'

Like Captain Marsh, Internee No 27006 T. E. Walter experienced the two extremes of prison existence—too little and too much to do. Like him, he saw little of his captors during the earlier stages of his captivity. Towards the end, also working on a 'death-railway', he went in constant dread of brutish Japanese guards armed with bamboos.

Born in Belize, British Honduras, in 1915, Tom Walter had gone to Sarawak, Borneo, in 1938 as a Divisional Forest Officer in the service of the 'White Rajah', Sir Charles Vyner Brooke. This was his first appointment since graduating in forestry at Edinburgh University, and he was not then married. On Boxing Day 1941, in a bid to escape the Japanese whose armies were by now sweeping through Malaya, he and a group of about twenty-five other Europeans, including women and children, set off on a hazardous journey across Borneo, shooting monsoon-swollen rapids in canoes, foot-slogging through jungle and over mountains. About two months and over 500 gruelling miles later, five of them reached Samarinda to find an unexpected aeroplane about to take off for Java. It seemed like a miraculous escape but, in Walter's case, luck did not hold.

In Batavia, capital of Java, he joined the RNVR but after a

few days went down with a bad attack of malaria. It was this that prevented his getting away when the shock news came that Java had capitulated, and on 14 April 1942, rounded up by the Japanese with all the other English civilians in Batavia, he heard clanging behind him the big black doors of Struiswijk Prison.

Walter's fellow-internees during the next 3½ years included some 200 English civilians based in Java—businessmen in Anglo-Dutch companies of all grades from General Manager down, managers and assistants from the tea, rubber and sisal plantations, Cable and Wireless employees, and some, like himself, who had just happened to be in Java owing to the hazards of war, including merchant seamen whose ships had been sunk. Categories were even wider among the much larger Dutch contingent and included a number of government officials.

Civilian internees naturally lacked the ingrained sense of discipline and camaraderie to be found in a POW camp, but Walter's account indicates a real communal effort to combat the twin enemies of boredom and hunger. Only when conditions became really grim did 'one-upmanship' assert itself, with a clique of 'camp officials' jockeying for privileged positions and black markets rampant in clothes, watches and other exploitable commodities.

During his eighteen months at Struiswijk, a prison built for 700, now housing 1,500, internees were locked in their cells from 6.30 pm till 7.30 next morning (the electric light kept on all night) and Walter occupied much of his time learning Dutch and chess. Chief event every day was the afternoon handball game ('the enthusiasm and skill which the game evoked was astonishing'). Main highlights were concerts given by a number of professional musicians, 'cabarets' produced by personnel from the Nirom broadcasting station, and talks given by any internee who had something interesting to say ('I did my bit with an hour's talk on "Across Darkest Borneo" ').

Walter describes the Japanese Commander at this camp as 'as near to being a gentleman as any Jap can be. He left us very much alone, and on his inspection rounds he was at least good enough to salute when we stood to attention. When we were suddenly told one September day in 1943 that all the British and the more important Dutch officials were to be taken elsewhere and must be ready to march out at midnight for an undisclosed destination, the Commander gave a touching speech of farewell and, while crocodile tears welled up in his eyes, asked forgiveness for his having had to keep us in prison.'

The next five months Walter spent in Soekamiskin Prison, Bandoeng, in tolerable conditions that made the more shocking his transference to a sprawling barracks on the other side of the town, at Tjimahi. As other batches of internees began to arrive from all over Java, it became apparent that the Japanese had decided to concentrate all civilians in Bandoeng, dispensing entirely with their services in helping to run the country. Eventually, despite protests about gross overcrowding, over 10,000 civilians were packed into the barrack blocks.

'All that separated us from the outside world was a thin matting fence and a few strands of barbed wire. In a country like Java, however, where Europeans would be conspicuous for miles, that was more than enough to deter us from trying to escape. The death penalty was promptly imposed as a further deterrent, and though this was never imposed, the few temporary escapees who went out to get some food got such a terrific beating up on their return after a short absence that no one ever again seriously considered escape.

'Most of the time I was quartered in one of the numerous long "wings", in which about eighty of us slept on the floor side by side. Our floor space varied according to how many were sick in hospital, but it was usually about 2 ft 6 inches wide. After the comparative comfort of Soekamiskin, we did not appreciate the continuous noise and bustle and complete lack of privacy.

'It soon became evident that the policy of the Japs as regards their treatment of us had undergone a radical change, and we soon began to long for the "hardships" of our previous prisons, which were luxurious hotels by comparison. Although the so-called Commandant was, I think, a sergeant, and a mysterious captain (responsible for all the camps in the Bandoeng area) occasionally put in an appearance, we were now, astonishing as it may seem, virtually in the hands of two or three common soldiers. They may well have been specially picked for their vicious and brutal qualities, and as it was practically impossible to get complaints past them to higher authorities, we were to all intents and purposes left to their tender mercies.

'For the first time the full Japanese military salute was now enforced—that is, if a Jap appeared in a building, the nearest internee had to shout out "kiutske" (attention!), then "kiri" (bow!), then "nauri" (straighten up!), and finally, when he'd gone, "jasmi" (dismiss!). Outside in the grounds the procedure was similar, and the progress of a Jap was accompanied by a wave of shouting—the official danger area when this rigmarole had to be undergone beginning and ending when the Jap was ten paces away. Needless to say, one was expected to have eyes in the back of one's head, and the well-worn excuse of unfortunates when they were arraigned that they "didn't see him" held as little water as the one that he was "more than ten paces away". "Insufficient respect" was always being used as an excuse for a general strafe, or a terrific beating up of some unfortunate individual.

'The "beatings up" varied from a few smacks in the face (returned in one famous case by an old man) to sadistical orgies in which the victim was literally half killed. After being knocked about till he was unconscious with anything that was handy (a log of wood, a rifle or bamboo sticks specially made for the purpose were the commonest articles used), he would be revived with buckets of water and the procedure would be continued till the Jap was too tired for any more. Another favourite punishment was to tie the unfortunate victim with his wrists behind his back, and suspend him from them so that his feet just didn't touch the ground, leaving him hanging there for several hours.

'Tortures involving more subtle technique, including the "water cure", burning with cigarette ends, and driving bamboo splinters under the fingernails, were reserved for the "kempe tai", or secret police. Usually these only dealt with political prisoners, but they were always being held up to us as bogey men by the Jap guards, who themselves lived in mortal terror of them. The "beating up" system is, of course, practised universally in the Jap army, and punishment is handed down through the various grades of officers until eventually the culprit is reached. Their alternative method of enforcing discipline is to punish everyone in the community for an individual's offence—examples in our case being the removal of all our books for some months, and a day's complete starvation.

'Another practice now enforced was ARP. Each block had to have two men permanently on duty throughout the night. Sitting down was considered an extremely serious offence, and as the Japs occasionally came round in the middle of the night, we had to keep a sharp look-out. Numerous other regulations with even less object were introduced periodically. Amongst the more permanent ones was the enforcing of the Japanese custom of walking barefoot inside the building and leaving our clogs (the universal footwear) at the entrance. A rule that caused a lot of trouble was the one forbidding people to smoke in the grounds of the camp unless they carried an ash tray and meticulously knocked off the ash into it. Perhaps the most ridiculous of all, though, was the fly swatting fatigue, introduced as a measure for keeping down flies. Each block leader had to carry solemnly down to the office his block's daily quota of swatted flies, which the various section leaders had collected from every individual. The number of corpses required per day varied with the size of the room—in one case fifty had somehow to be produced. We were, of course, made to buy the necessary fly-swats from the Japs.

'The food situation in this camp started by being bad and, with only a few bright intervals, got steadily worse and worse. This steady deterioration was partly caused by the fact that, although the price of foodstuffs was soaring, the official daily feeding allowance of 25 cents per man was never altered. The situation became desperate in about September 1944 when our weekly meat ration of five buffaloes was cut out, the daily bread became a sort of doughy bun (owing to shortage of yeast) and the purchase of foodstuffs extra to our basic ration of 100 grams of rice per day was curtailed to a negligible quantity. Bacillary dysentery and hunger oedema became widespread. From a normal eleven stone I reached a record low of eight stone, and fainted on three occasions.

'There were plenty of Dutch doctors but, with practically no medicines available, there wasn't much they could do. The mortality rate was highest in the 50–60 age group, and though the number of deaths was never published, the death rate must have been very high. On looking back now, the surprising thing is not that so many died, but that so many lived.

'In June 1945 the Japs suddenly announced that we had to produce two thousand men for building a railway somewhere in Java. To make the proposition as attractive as possible, they announced that those going would be "fed up" on double rations for a month beforehand, and that, though the work would be hard, there would be plenty of food. I was caught in this net, and after a short period of the so-called double rations we were moved off, in tightly shuttered railway carriages, to a village on the eastern edge of the plain of Bandoeng. From there, carrying our pathetic belongings as best we could, we were herded along an apparently never-ending road to our destination.

'Here we had a foretaste of what was in store for us when we were "welcomed" to a parade outside the camp by a crowd of the most degenerate specimens of humanity I have yet seen. They were all suitably armed with bamboos, with which they were not slow in demonstrating their proficiency at the expense of stragglers. I had barely recovered from an attack of dysentery, and the combination of exhaustion and extreme heat caused me to celebrate my arrival by being violently sick.

'No preparations had been made to receive us and it was not until late at night that we received a cup of tea for our evening meal. We were roused at 5 am and were not exactly encouraged by the announcement that this was purely a working camp, and that owing to our period of double rations we were all supposed to be healthy. Accordingly sickness was "strictly forbidden" and under all circumstances we would have to send out 1,900 men every day. This was no idle threat, as we subsequently discovered, for on days when our ranks of moderately able-bodied men were depleted by sickness, they were speedily filled by persuasive methods applied by the Japs to any unfortunates they might find. Whether they could even walk, much less do a day's work, was immaterial.

'The camp in which we were quartered consisted merely of a number of disused brick-drying sheds. There was no adequate sanitation and all water for drinking or washing had to be carried from a well some distance outside the camp, so that very strict rationing was necessary. Medical facilities were practically non-existent, and the most one could expect by being sick was half-rations, an occasional cup of water, and a good chance of being beaten out to work. In fact the general conditions were so appalling that the one thing that saved this "corvee" from becoming the "death-railway" it was obviously intended to be was the fact that the weather was perfect, and not a drop of rain fell during the whole five weeks we were there.

'The work here consisted of building a railway from Tjitjilengka to Madjelaya—both villages of no importance in the middle of nowhere. The track of this had already been marked out, and in some places a cutting of about twenty feet deep had to be made, while in others an embankment as much as twenty feet high was necessary. In some parts we were working in wet *sawahs* (flooded rice fields) with water a foot deep, and sinking into the deep mud beneath. On this sort of terrain we had to make embankments of mud dug out with our hands from the adjoining *sawahs*, or of dry earth which we carried some distance in baskets, or passed along in a human chain. The fate awaiting the first train to run along this line—had it ever been completed—was conjectured on with some amusement.

'A typical day would start at 5 am with a bowl of watery rice mixed with bits of rotten sweet potatoes, followed at about 6 by tea. We were divided into working parties of 100 men with a Jap in charge of each, and trudged out as dawn was breaking, feeling half frozen. Lunch consisted of about a pound of "bread" which was so bitter that it required a considerable effort to get it down. We were allowed to buy (through the Japs) fermented sticks of tapioca, which had a faint alcoholic flavour, and occasionally a duck egg at 5 guilders (10s 6d). With the need for money now greater than ever, the clothing racket started again. For those who had no clothes to dispose of, it was just too bad, and I personally found that the only way of scraping up a small income to cover an occasional duck egg and the daily tapioca, was by selling half my bread ration—a whole loaf fetched from 3 to 7 guilders. It was not surprising in these conditions that most of the doubtful characters in the camp somehow managed to wangle jobs in the kitchen, where they made full use of their opportunities.

'It was after some five weeks of this slave driving that the welcome announcement was made that we would not be required to go out for the next few days. When this was followed by a Jap officer striking the flag at the camp, and (I heard) his stamping it on the ground, the inference to be drawn that the war was over sent us wild with joy. No official announcement was made to that effect, but when a week later we were sent back to Tjimahi, our suspicions were confirmed by the natives who cheered us on our walk to the station.

'The first official announcement that the war was over was by a proclamation from the Emperor posted up shortly afterwards, which read roughly as follows: "Owing to repeated requests from the Allies, and in order to save further bloodshed, His Imperial Majesty, the Emperor, has graciously given his consent for hostilities to cease." Many of the Japs in Java may have been deluded into thinking that they had won the war, but we certainly weren't.

'The next six weeks were just one gigantic binge. Not only were the camp rations increased at least four-fold, but we were able to go out to the local village and buy anything we wanted. Practically every day the Japs issued clothing and cigarettes from their army stocks, and we promptly sold these outside at fantastic prices. Thus we could afford all the ducks' eggs, fruit and buffalo meat we could manage—the daily routine as far as I was concerned being a visit to the village in the morning to load up with stocks, followed by a prolonged session sitting over a fire putting my culinary skill to practice.

'On 1 October all the British were sent down by train to Batavia, from whence, a few days later, we were evacuated by plane to Singapore—free at last.'

7 *Love and War*

During the terrible autumn of 1940, when German bombs rained down on London for seventy-six consecutive nights, Joan Veazey, newly married to the young curate of a church near the Elephant and Castle, kept a 'wrist-diary' of the happenings around her. The notes she jotted down on a pad attached by a rubber band to her wrist were later transcribed and incorporated into a 35,000-word journal she entitled 'Love and War'.

It is a spontaneous and highly personal record of the London Blitz, inspired less by the undaunted spirit of Cockneys 'taking it' than by devotion to the husband she adored. Christopher Veazey was the son of Canon H. G. Veazey, Vicar of St Mark's Church, Camberwell, for fifty-two years, and to him the drab streets and tenements of south-east London were familiar territory. To his pretty young bride, brought up in a happily conventional middle-class family, they remained disturbingly alien. Even her first visit to her future father-in-law's vicarage near the Old Kent Road had shocked her: 'The street littered with all sorts of rubbish—orange peel, chocolate papers, bits of vegetable leaves—the house lofty and rather dark, the "grounds" tired grass and a patch of asphalt in the front.'

Although the diary gives some memorable glimpses of the Blitz in one of London's worst-hit working-class districts, the workers themselves remain shadowy figures, a few 'characters' apart. What is most touchingly revealed is the impact of those harrowing, chaotic months on the young diarist herself, suddenly transplanted from a cosy, predictable suburbia into a world of bombs and squalor. All the dreams cherished through her long engagement go up in smoke—the white wedding a macabre hustle to the strains of droning planes and gunfire, the honeymoon two months delayed, shattering glass and blown-in doors the accompaniment to setting up house.

But love does prove stronger than war. Even on the last and worst night of the Blitz, when their church is going up in flames and all their efforts to quell the inferno seem like 'a thimbleful of water on to Hell itself', she is buoyed up by the knowledge that she is now carrying Christopher's child. 'Sometimes I wonder if my baby will be born with a stirrup-pump in its hand!'

Joan Veazey's parents had lost everything in the Slump in the early 1930s and, when the journal opens, in 1937, her mother was running a Guest House in Sutton and Joan, who had had a public school and art school education, was posing as an artist's model (several costume portraits of her were exhibited at the Royal Academy).

In September 1937 Christopher Veazey, a 25-year-old curate at a nearby church, joined the seven other lodgers—'dark hair, brown eyes, rather like a gypsy, quiet and a bit shy but with a charming smile and very interesting voice'. They fell in love and he proposed two months later. Joan's only worry was whether she would ever make a good parson's wife—'I feel certain I will shock the Parish!' Soon Christopher was given a new curacy at St Mary's Church, near the Elephant and Castle. Three months before the war they went on a climbing holiday together in the Swiss Alps with Canon and Mrs Veazey.

It was not until 14 September 1940, shortly after sporadic raids had developed into a full-scale Blitz, that they were finally married, at St Mary's Church, Kennington. For Joan, coming from the comparative safety of the suburbs, conditions under the Blitz were a revelation. They drove from her home in a hired car. In a large crate on top of the car was the wedding cake, 'very large and flat with a very intricate design worked out on the panels, the initials of bride and groom on one panel and icing matching the gown'. The wedding gown, of parchment satin, was the sixteenth she had tried on—'I felt quite unashamed of my delight as I stood before the mirror.'

'As we got nearer to London, I noticed the damage that had been done during the week's raids. Buildings reduced to heaps of rubble. In some parts the Wardens were still helping the rescue teams to find the victims. It was a terrible sight to witness on my wedding day! Some houses were still smouldering and the smell was sickening. A few of the roads were impassable, being blocked with craters or fenced off for unexploded bombs. I wondered what we were going to do, for I had never seen anything like this before.

'When we arrived at the Rectory, where we were to live until we found a place of our own, the Rector showed us the safest room that he could find for us. It was actually the butler's kitchen years ago and it was lined with sinks and cupboards. There were two divans in it and one chair. Wooden shutters covered the windows and the room was not furnished with any curtains. We didn't mind a scrap—for this was our wedding room and somehow we would make it look nice.

'I started by scrubbing the floor. It took ages, for I was not used to doing it and it seemed terribly hard. Then I bought the last packet of crepe paper from the little shop over the way. It was a frightful royal blue, a really gaudy colour. I made some frilly curtains from it and stuck them up with drawing pins.

'While I was doing this Christopher took two weddings for the Rector, and he went to see the Lady Doctor to ask her if she would let us use her house for the wedding preparations. She was so kind and also promised to give us all a Wedding Tea afterwards. We finished making the room look tidy and then we took our wedding clothes and the cake along to the Doctor's house.

'After this we went along to see the School keeper and we spent a little while sheltering from the raids in the boiler room! We had a cup of tea and went back to have lunch with the Doctor's family. After lunch I rested and had a hot bath. Then I started dressing in the loveliest of gowns. The veil was so beautiful that I was almost afraid to touch it. I wondered if any other brides can say that they have scrubbed a floor on their wedding day, had tea in a coal hole, and made paper curtains for the marriage room!

'As soon as I was ready, the Doctor drove me and my father in her car, and I was driven to the Church with my Father who had arrived a few minutes earlier. My Mother and Christopher's Mother were waiting for us, and Mother took a snap of me as I stepped from the car.

'It was very disappointing inside the Church for no one had switched the lights on, and the Church was deserted except for about six people who were at the other end. Christopher's Father and a Server carrying the processional Cross walked towards me, and my Father whispered to me that he was nervous! I was far too thrilled to worry about being like that. We walked down to the Chancel steps and I found Christopher there to join me. As I came to him he gave me a lovely smile—one that I shall never forget. And he was standing so that a shaft of sunlight came down on him. I knew then that I loved him even more than I thought.

'There was no music, and all my dreams of a big wedding were broken, but I did not mind for at last I was to be Christopher's for ever. As his Father gave us the Blessing, the siren sounded again its dreadful howling notes. Christopher took my hand and lifted my veil to kiss me. It gave me such confidence that I did not feel frightened. We walked to the vestry and out into the Rectory garden. There while the planes were battling in a life and death struggle overhead we stood quietly for our photographs to be taken.

'Suddenly, without any warning a German plane flew in low over the house and released a bomb. I shouted to the photographer who was under the black velvet cloth trying to take the photo, "Look out, he's dropping bombs." The man just shouted back from the cloth, "Never mind about the bomb—just SMILE." One of the bombs fell quite near, hitting a Church a little way up the road. My veil was torn when I tried to get to shelter in our Church. As we walked down the nave to the drone of planes and the noise of gunfire overhead, I heard Christopher's Mother trying to whistle the wedding march for us. Even she realised how we longed for all the trimmings.

'We went to tea at the Doctor's house and cut the cake. Then we posed in the front garden for a few snaps, which my Mother took. As we waited there a fire engine came rushing along and, as it slowed up a little to turn the corner, I threw a flower from my lovely bouquet which one of the men on the engine caught, and blew a kiss back.

'Later we went back to the Rectory and, having changed out of our wedding clothes, set about tidying our room. I scrubbed the shelves and cupboards while Christopher fixed up a string for our clothes and unpacked the few things we had brought with us. We have two divan beds, one of which we have turned on its side between the windows and ourselves. It should be some protection from flying glass.

'It's getting dark and the siren has just gone again. Christopher is upstairs in the kitchen on the third floor boiling a kettle for a final cup of tea and filling some flasks in case we need them during the night. The Rector is coming in a few minutes for some supper—tea and wedding cake.

'*15 September, Sunday.* What a terrible night it has been. Although the warning had gone there was little to hear except an occasional plane droning overhead and the "bark" of guns trying to hit it. We settled down on our small divan bed wearing our fire-fighting suits, Christopher in slacks and pullover and I in his old ski suit. I think Christopher must have dozed, but I lay awake, tense and nervous every time there was a bang outside. Then quite suddenly it began. The guns blazed away and bombs began to fall, sometimes singly, sometimes in sticks of half a dozen or so. I clutched hold of Christopher as one explosion seemed particularly near, and he woke up. He held me tightly for a moment, got out of bed and put on his shoes, and then in again. He told me that he didn't fancy walking about on broken glass in his socks so I put mine on too. It seemed an eternity before things quietened down and we dozed fitfully off.

'Suddenly there was a loud knocking on our door. I called out, "Come in", and one of the Parishioners, who is sleeping in the huge basement kitchen across the passage, came to tell us that she thought we ought to get up as the house was on fire with an incendiary bomb on the top floor. Christopher went up to see what he could do to help and I followed him up the steep spiral staircase. When we got to the top we found a small group of people standing round a pile of earth and sand which looked rather like a Christmas pudding in the middle of the landing. Blue flames were spluttering from the pile and every time anyone poked it flames shot up the wall almost to the ceiling. Christopher took one look at it, shovelled it into a bucket of sand and carried it downstairs in double quick time and threw it into the garden.

'After making sure we had put the woodwork out we went back to our room but we were too wide awake to get to sleep. So we poured out tea from the flasks and had some more wedding cake till the All Clear sounded at 5.30 am. Christopher had an early Service and must have felt very tired after such a wedding night.

'There have been a great many raids all day. In fact, it has been almost continuous. At times we have seen planes coming down in flames—and the white lines of their exhausts turning into pitch black smoke as the planes are hit. I can hardly believe that I have been married for 24 hours and in spite of the war raging over us, I quite like it. When I told Christopher this a few minutes ago he replied dryly, "It's just as well you do, because we can't be unmarried now."

'The siren has gone again and I have been getting the large kitchen across the passage ready for the three families who shelter there at night. They are a happy crowd. There is a bus conductor and his wife, a policeman, his wife and daughter and an elderly pensioner—who refuses to take his overcoat and cap off even for sleeping! It is rather nice having them with us at night because all the men take turns to patrol the house, Church and Hall for two hours at a stretch, leaving everyone else free to sleep if they can. If the man on patrol finds anything wrong, as last night, he calls all the others to help. Christopher is on patrol from 2 till 4 am when he calls the Rector to take over from him. I expect I shall be with him as I worry when he is away. I am dreading tonight. Last night was new and exciting to me, but I am not at all sure if I will like it every night. I hope I shall stick it for Christopher's sake. The others seem to look up to me not to show any fear.

'*16 September.* Another bad night, with bombs falling and guns firing incessantly. Christopher and I were on patrol at 2 am. At one time he disappeared and I thought I should never find him again. It is a huge house and I don't know how many rooms. To make matters worse only a few of the rooms are blacked out and none of the halls, landings or stairs, so that we have to patrol in pitch darkness, using a small dimmed torch. It is very eerie going round the rooms on the top floor when the guns are blazing and a plane seems to be hovering just over the roof. Then from time to time we went across to the Church and hall to see that everything was safe there. The worst incident of the night was when a mouse dropped into my frizzy hair whilst I was asleep. Its struggles and squeals for help woke me up. I was so sleepy that when I put my hand up and felt it a cold shudder went down my back.

'They must have broken the gas and water mains last night because there is no gas and no water. Luckily we have an oil stove on which we can make tea and for the rest we have to put up with cold things and vegetables cooked over an ordinary coal fire. We went to the Doctor's for lunch and found she was existing on cold tinned foods.

'Tonight we have been round some of the shelters on our visits. It is amazing what discomfort people will put up with. Some of them spend the night on mattresses, others in deck chairs and some even lying on concrete floors wrapped in a couple of blankets. In nearly all the shelters the atmosphere is so thick that you could almost cut it with a knife. Quite frankly, some even stink! I think I should prefer to risk death in the open rather than asphyxiation. I was amazed to see mothers breast feeding their babies and young couples making love surrounded by others washing themselves in dirty little bowls and using buckets surrounded by canvas screens. After these had been used by two hundred or so people the results are pretty appalling.

'*17 September*. We didn't have a moment's rest last night. The Germans came over in waves. There was a full moon and we heard the queer drone as they came. Then the thuds, first far away and then nearer and nearer. It was quite terrifying though I didn't let Christopher see that I was frightened. We saw the strangest sights this morning. Some quite well dressed people going to work as best they could—on lorries, in carts and on top of taxis. The Londoners are not willing to be put off by the Germans. There have been many terrible casualties by bombing but we cannot know the numbers yet because the press keep everything so vague in case of giving the enemy any information.

'We have had another basket of fire-bombs. They are horrid things, for the more you put earth on them the more they seem to frizzle and flame. The light is so bright that it hurts your eyes to look at them. I put one out tonight—with a tin hat!

'*18 September*. I was busy frying the breakfast egg this morning when I noticed through the window a German plane coming in to bomb. Suddenly I saw three black blobs leave the plane. I landed flat on my tummy, still holding the frying pan—and I didn't spill a drop of fat! The Rector came out of the dining room to see if I had hurt myself and he was startled to see me on the floor. 'Hello, Joan. What are you doing there?" "I'm cooking your breakfast, Rector!" was all I could gasp.

'I now realise that I have been living in a fool's paradise in Sutton and never understood what a ghastly time they were having in London. But now *I* am a Londoner—and I'm feeling so very proud of being in it all with Christopher.

'*19 September.* This afternoon we went to see Christopher's parents and found them looking very happy in spite of a great deal of damage from bombs all around their house. We had a lovely bath followed by a rest and sleep soon after we arrived. We get very tired with work all day and the anxious worry of the nightly air-raids. My darling has been so wonderful to me. He is a perfect husband and I could not wish for a dearer man. After tea, we went back to the Rectory to get ready for tonight.

'After the siren had gone we went along to the Elephant and Castle tube shelter to see some of the people who were sheltering there. I had no idea there would be so many people down there. They were lying closely packed along all the corridors and passages and even on the platforms, so that people who wanted to board the trains had to step over mattresses, cases and sleeping bodies. There was a general atmosphere almost like a picnic with families eating their suppers of fish and chips, while others were singing loudly. Tiny babies were tucked up in suitcases and small children were toddling about quite unconcerned in the draughty, unpleasant atmosphere. We talked to some of the groups but could not do very much as there were so many hundreds down there. The noise was appalling.

'*20 September.* I have worked hard today and I feel happy because every time I get my hands really dirty I know I am doing it for Christopher, because I love him and want to be a fine wife to him.

'The planes are hovering overhead and we are feeling very tense. I wonder what sort of night it is going to be.

'22 *September, Sunday.* I went to church at 6.30. It is amazing how people turn up in spite of the bombing. Some people say they feel safe in church. I wonder what it would be like if a bomb fell close by? The tons of masonry would fall and crush every one of us attending the service. No, I don't feel safe anywhere.

'27 *September.* Our day off. We went down to Sutton and I spent the afternoon having a perm to strengthen my morale.

'28 *September.* We slept in a real bed last night for the first time since we were married. And in comparison with London the night was calm. It's wonderful to see houses which can still boast that they have all their windows in, and no piles of broken panes in every road. We came back in time for Christopher to take a wedding in the afternoon and, like ours, it was interrupted by an air raid.

'13 *October, Sunday.* After the evening service the congregation met together for a cup of tea and at the same time presented Christopher with a cheque for his wedding present. We are not going to spend it till things quieten down a bit and we can make a home of our own. A cosy evening with the Rector in our little room drinking tea and eating biscuits. The wedding cake has all gone.

'14 *October.* The sirens have gone. We are down in our room again. Our guns are going full-pelt and the Jerrys are overhead. A few minutes ago we went to patrol the church hall. Outside it was nearly as bright as day with a full moon shining and, to add to the light, the pilots dropped four very large flares, one almost overhead. They should be able to see everything they want tonight.

'We had a job to do this evening: to take an old gentleman, a Mr Edwards, back to hospital where he had been for three weeks. He and his wife are very old and were quite unable to care for themselves, so they had gone into hospital and now he has discharged himself. We found him sitting on a stool on the pavement outside his house looking drawn and unhappy. He was determined to carry on by himself, but he had no food or drink in the house except for a jug of drinking water which had turned green and a bottle of milk which had been there for three weeks. After a long talk with him, we persuaded him to go back to hospital with us in a taxi.

'*16 October*. Last night was the worst we have had—at least that is how it seemed to me. Christopher and I can manage to sleep through quite a lot, now that it has been going on for over a month, but neither of us had much sleep. The noise from the guns hardly ceased and on one occasion the front door was burst open by the vibration of a large gun firing from the streets opposite the house.

'We have just heard that one of the large trench shelters in the park received a direct hit. They are still digging and there are all sorts of rumours going around as to how many people are trapped there. We know that one of our families from the church, who go there to shelter every night, has not come home. So far there is no news. There is nothing we can do but wait and pray for all those who are listening for the scratch of the shovels as the rescue party gets nearer to them.

'*17 October*. We have heard that they have found the Pottles who were in the park shelter. If what we hear is true, they were seated along the wall of the trench knitting and reading when there was a sudden blue flash and the earth and concrete caved in on them all. The parents and their son are safe and in hospital but their daughter, who was one of our Sunday School teachers, died from shock and her injuries soon after they rescued her. Christopher hopes to go and see the others in hospital soon. We still do not know how many were killed but it must be a very big number for a great part of the shelter collapsed.

'*24 October*. The Rector has gone away for a week's holiday and left us in charge. I hope nothing happens while he is away—I should hate to have to write to tell him that his home no longer existed.

'*25 October.* Jerry must have known that the Rector had gone, because we had another bad time last night. Just after we had settled down to sleep, a stick of six bombs landed very close to us, one of them hitting a shelter behind the little shops on the other side of the road. We went over to see of we could help, but everything was soon under control. It was rather eerie to see the blue glimmer of the ambulance light creeping along and then stopping. I heard that eight people were killed.

'*26 October.* We are in the middle of a very nasty night and so far none of us have had a wink of sleep. At 7 o'clock I went over to the little chemist shop opposite to collect a paraffin stove which we had lent and, while I chatted, the chemist asked me to stay and have a cup of tea and a cigarette. At that moment the siren went and, since they seemed rather jumpy, I suggested that they could pack up and come over to us with the stove. They seemed glad to accept and said they would be over in half an hour. I told them they could shelter in the wine cellar under the stairs every night if they liked.

'It didn't take us long to clean out the wine cellar and to put blankets and a mattress on the floor for them. By the time we had finished getting ready they came over, and we settled down with the other shelterers for tea and talk. Suddenly, at about eight o'clock, there was a terrific explosion which filled the Rectory with dust, smoke and smells. The shutters and frames of the windows split and burst open. There followed a moment of absolute silence while we wondered whether the house was beginning to fall on top of us. I grabbed a flask of tea and ran into the old kitchen where a number of our shelterers were looking dusty and dazed. I shouted "Does anyone want a nice cuppa?" And it did the trick! Then we went to the two in the wine cellar and found that the man was having a heart attack. Christopher went for the Doctor while I gave him a drink of sal volatile.

'When Christopher came back with the Doctor a few minutes later, he took me aside and told me that the bomb had landed on the rear of the chemist's shop exactly opposite the front door.

The shop itself was now a heap of rubble. I didn't know how to break the news so I waited till they asked me where the bomb had landed. I replied, "If a bomb landed on the pub next door to your home, what would happen?" The chemist said, "My little place would never stand up to it." I leaned over to him and said very quietly, "I am sorry old chap, but it wasn't on the pub." I thought for a moment that he was going to have another attack, but luckily the injections which the Doctor had given him had done the trick.

'*Later.* We have had a difficult time trying to fix up some blackout to enable us to turn the lights on. It is dreadfully cold because there is not a pane of glass left in the house. We haven't even tried to find the front door yet so we hope no one will walk in during the night. Christopher is over in the church trying to clean the worst of the mess up for the early service tomorrow morning (or is it this morning?). Dear Rector you knew a thing or two when you took this week off.

'*27 October, Sunday.* As Christopher went over to the Service at eight o'clock, he ran back to ask me to tidy the front garden, adding "You will need a ladder!" When I got outside I found half the contents of the chemist's shop scattered all over the front garden and, to my horror, the one and only tree was festooned with sanitary towels which were hanging by their loops! To the accompaniment of shrill and lewd whistles from passers-by, I had to retrieve them one by one. Later Christopher returned the till of the shop which had been blown right across the main road into the porch of the church. There were crowds of people picking up anything they could find which they thought might be of value. It is horrible to see them coming down like Vultures on someone's misfortune.

'This morning we had twelve bombed-out folk to breakfast. They came so gratefully and the fresh tea, although dusty, cheered them all. It was little to do but it helped. After breakfast I took over huge jugs of hot tea to the rescue party who were trying to see what could be salvaged out of the debris. Just as they had finished, a canteen van drew up and I was politely ticked off by a superior lady in charge. Oh! These official minds!

'*28 October.* It is getting very cold in the Rectory today. We have cleared up most of the mess made by the bomb which fell opposite and have rehung the front door. But there is not a pane of glass left in the house. It is quite impossible to fix the window linen which the wardens have brought round because all the window frames are of metal. We must hope that the Rector will have some glass fixed when he gets home.

'I have been working over at the dairy opposite this afternoon helping the dairyman to clear his shop. It is completely shattered and will have to come down. He and his wife are making plans for returning to Wales to start life afresh.

'*1 November.* The Rector arrived home early and he took the damage very lightly. Nothing seems to worry him. I have never met a man so calm in danger and so completely without fear. One evening I found him sitting in his study quite unconcerned though the shutters had been bent right in with blast.

'Christopher and I are still trying to deal with old Mr Edwards. We found him at his bombed home walking up and down reciting a long poem of the sea. He told us of his youth when he was a sea captain and how he used to chase smugglers. The poem contained over forty verses and he was apparently word-perfect. He and his wife are now out of hospital but they cannot stay at their flat till it is mended, so we have brought them along to the Rectory. We hope to get them settled in a day or so.

'*5 November.* We have had fireworks of another kind today. Guns blazing at enemy planes overhead. We all pretend to be as cool as cucumbers but is there anyone who can say truthfully "I am not frightened"? Perhaps our dear Rector could, but I have never met anyone else so fearless. Tonight we have had a few facts given to us by the press. Fourteen thousand people have been killed since the Blitz first started.

'We asked the Rector if we could have our belated honeymoon soon. He has given us permission to go for a week, probably about the 19th. Christopher simply can't understand why I like to have new things to wear for this great occasion. He always looks so fine in his Priest's uniform, but my few things are getting very worn.

'*7 November*. The siren wailed at 7 pm and since we heard it we have counted seventeen bombs. My father-in-law has given me a new tin hat. At last I have my own tin hat instead of wearing my large saucepan!

'*9 November*. News has come through that Neville Chamberlain died in the night. He must have overworked and died of a broken heart. He spoke of his wife during his lifetime as being a wonderful Wife, Friend and Companion. He was very devoted to her and his love will surely live on in her heart.

'*10 November, Sunday*. We had the Cadets in church this day. The organist played the Funeral March in honour of our late Prime Minister. There are many bombs dropping whilst I write this. I have counted over twenty already.

'*19 November*. Our honeymoon day! We dressed very early and finished our packing. I suppose that when a woman marries she thinks that her man is the most wonderful one in the world. The only difference between us is that I KNOW my husband is the best! There is not a breath I take without inwardly thanking God for Christopher.

'We went to Paddington and to our surprise found Mr Evans, the dairyman from opposite us, waiting there complete with a bag of confetti to see us off. We arrived at Llandudno Junction at 4 pm. From there our little train chugged along to Betws-y-Coed and stopped at nearly every station. At one stop an old man slung a huge bunch of dead rabbits in and then struggled in himself. I think he had been drinking.

'We arrived at the hotel in time for dinner. After we had revelled in the glories of a hot bath, we changed into evening dress and walked down to the dining room. I was delighted to see that Christopher had thought to order a bottle of champagne. We are creatures of habit, for I felt out of place in my long evening gown instead of the usual garb of tin hat and slacks. After dinner we retired to a wonderful feather bed and twelve hours of solid sleep.

'20 *November*. We have had a lovely night of real rest. It was a joy to wake up in a lovely nightgown instead of those serge trousers. Those clean sheets . . . and the coolness of Wales in the early morning. Christopher went for a long walk over the hills. It was good that he felt the need for his favourite pastime. After lunch we went for a walk to see the Swallow Falls. They seemed rather cruel this time, for I had only seen them in the summer before. We stood as close as we dared and watched in silence.

'On our return we went upstairs to enjoy more lounging in hot water—so hot that it was iron-coloured as it left the tap. By the time we had cooled it down the bath was nearly overflowing. I went to bed early in order to make the most of the precious hours of sleep which will be impossible when we return to the Elephant and Castle.

'21 *November*. We didn't get up till nearly nine this morning, for the big double bed was so very cosy . . . and it was our honeymoon.

'22 *November*. We went with some of the other guests to Llandudno and we talked of London all the way there.

'23 *November*. Christopher took me to see the Fairy Glen, and then asked me to go swimming in those rapids, so that he could tell those at home that he really did see the fairy!

'24 *November, Sunday*. I think I am getting worried about going back to all the hell of the bombs, for I have been ill today.

'25 *November*. I am still in bed, feeling pretty grim. I am certain it's sheer panic about going back.

'26 *November*. We were called at seven and had an early breakfast. Very slowly we walked to the train. I watched the hills as the train passed by. They looked darker and more lonely than when we came. The train seemed to go so quickly, and I felt my tummy turning over as I realised that soon we should hear that awful wailing siren again.

'When we arrived home, we found that our room had been brightened by some lovely flowers, and attached was a little card on which was written, "Welcome Home—from F.F.G., the Rector, Mrs Edney, and the Mice."

'*19 December.* At last, we have definitely got a flat! It's on the top floor, but who cares. If we are going to be bombed I would sooner be on top of the debris than underneath tons of masonry.

'*24 December.* Christopher took me to Peckham to buy some lino for the flat. It is expensive—nearly twelve pounds, but will last longer than the cheaper sort. This evening we have been very busy making curtains for the windows. Christopher does all the measuring and cutting, and I am sewing yards and yards of material on a borrowed machine.

'I wonder if Hitler is hanging up his stocking for OUR bombs!

'*25 December.* Thank goodness we are having a quiet Christmas. I bought a large chicken and we had a super Christmas dinner between the three of us. We tried to cheer up our Rector, but he was missing his wife terribly as she had been evacuated with their two daughters.

'*28 December.* All quiet. Is it a lull before a storm?

'*29 December, Sunday.* My God! I was right. We've had an awful night. HE's followed by hundreds of fire-bombs. The fires in the City cast a dark red glow over the whole of central London. And our flames must have looked the same from the City. My father-in-law's district had a land-mine that killed more than twenty people.

'Christopher and I dealt with about two dozen fire bombs which came down in the Rectory garden and on the roofs of the Church and Rectory. Christopher managed to squeeze himself through a small window of a disused stable and he put out a fire-bomb which was beginning to catch the wood of the stable alight. I managed to push a coal-hod full of earth through the window for Christopher to use on the bomb. I don't want another night like this for a long while. It was pretty grim.

'*13 January.* We have had a dreadful night. Bombs coming down so often that we really began to get frightened. There was a short lull when we tried to snatch a little rest, but we were suddenly tipped up at an angle of forty-five degrees from the divan. We found out afterwards that a time-bomb had exploded and killed three people at the end of the garden. We have lost nearly every pane of glass in this huge house once more. When will this war end?

'*15 January.* The RSPCA called for our kitten this afternoon. We have had to have it put to sleep as there is a rule in the flats that we are not allowed to keep pets.

'*18 January.* It is snowing today. I know because I have just had to sweep it off the dining room table with the crumb tray. We have no glass in the windows so the snow just flutters in and makes pretty patterns.

'*20 January.* We left the Rectory and set up in our own home—our flat! I wondered, as I climbed into the bed, how many folk had lived there before us. How many had loved, hated, or even lost their loved ones since this flat was first lived in, twenty years ago. The Rector's wife has come home to take charge of the Rectory.

'*8 March.* I have helped Christopher with two weddings. And tonight as I write this there is a raid going on. It is nasty and seems to be a special one for this district. Christopher and I have just been out to see if we can help where a few houses have been knocked down two doors away from the Rectory. There are many folk buried there.

'*Later.* The doctor asked me to take a few notes down for her. While I waited—she was hanging upside down in a small opening in order to give injections to the victims—I spent the time waving a large red lamp in the middle of the road to warn the trams and cars of the debris which was strewn across the road.

'It was rather a big bomb . . . and bombs make a nasty mess of blood, blackness and bandages.

'*14 March.* Six months of our lives together, and they have been wonderfully happy in spite of this wretched war. We have proved that Love and War live together.

'*26 March.* I am feeling rather queer today. I suppose it is the rushing about—sometimes on an empty tummy—that has caused this feeling.

'*29 March.* My unborn baby must be so tiny. It is amazing how a tiny thing can make one feel so ill. Perhaps the war will be over in nine months' time. Christopher is so looking forward to having a child of his own. I pray to God that I shall be able to carry it safely through all this devastation.

'*12 April.* A message by our Premier, Mr Winston Churchill: "I see the damage done by the enemy attacks; but I also see side by side with the devastation and amid the ruins quiet, confident, bright and smiling eyes, bearing up with a consciousness of being associated with a cause far higher and wider than any human personal issue. I see the Spirit of an unconquerable people."

'*16 April.* The warning has gone again. Every raid seems to get worse than the previous one. We have seen the most horrible sights tonight and experienced some dreadful hours. We had tried to sleep at the Rectory to fire-watch in our turns, but before we had even settled we heard the bombs falling, ghastly shrieking noises followed by sickening thuds. I believe someone once wrote in one of the papers that a true Christian's prayer was that the bomb would drop on him rather than on his fellow-men. I am not a Christian . . . I have counted over sixty bombs this night. Strange as it may seem I have felt much calmer this evening. Perhaps it is because I am bearing Christopher's child.

'*17 April.* I felt very fed up this morning. As usual after a bad raid there is no gas and little water. I had piled four saucepans on top of each other to try and cook on our small paraffin stove and, when all was set, a bomb fell quite near and sent my stew all over the floor of the flat. I just broke down and cried and, of course, Christopher had to come in soon after it had happened. When he saw the slimy, sticky mess of stew and vegetables, he laughed and said, "Where do we sit, darling?"

'*7 May.* There is a letter in the press today. It tells of the bravery of others and suggests that the clergy should be included in the lists. Certainly I know of many Clergy, including my own Christopher, who are more than brave.

'*10 May.* A terrible night—the worst blitz we have had. Our town is practically burnt out. Our lovely Church is merely a charred shell. We have seen the beams blazing furiously and then falling one by one, until the Altar caught alight and seemed to fold up and die before our eyes. The Church burnt with white hot flames. It was a dreadful sight, and though we tried hard in the beginning to get the fire under control, we failed hopelessly. The windows had gone, the wind changed its direction and fanned the flames to even greater heights. We could hear the cries of the pigeons in the tower of the Church, but we found it impossible to reach them. The Great Bells fell from the top of the tower with a mighty rush of sparks and flames.

'Christopher and I saved as much of the contents of the Church safe as we could, the old records of births, marriages and deaths. The silver and other valuables we piled on to the Rectory lawn. In our haste to do all we could before we were trapped, we forgot to bring out the beautiful kneelers and altar frontals which belonged to our Church. Somehow we were so terribly tired that we forgot to remove a great many things though we did save the Vestments.

'In spite of being pregnant I found strength enough to help by carrying over forty-two buckets of water from the tanks of the Rectory down the five flights of stairs and through the garden to the Church Tower entrance. My efforts were of no use whatever. It was like pouring a thimbleful of water on to Hell itself.

'When Christopher realised that we had lost our Church he decided that we should walk down towards the Elephant and Castle which had several nasty fires going. We tried to help at Spurgeon's Tabernacle, but this building had been burning for hours and it was impossible to save it. Soon we found someone who needed help. A row of houses had caught alight and there were only two men to help. Between us we managed to get the fire under control. Sometimes I wonder if my baby will be born with a stirrup-pump in its hand!'

Joan Veazey's daughter, Janet, was born in a nursing home, after a prolonged and painful confinement, on 15 December 1941. By then there was a real home to return to, the fifteen-room Vicarage they had moved into in August after Christopher had been inducted as Vicar of St Silas Church, Nunhead, half an hour's journey from the charred shell of their old church. The nursery walls had been painted pale blue with pale pink almond blossom painted at the corners by Uncle David Veazey. Mrs Veazey had embroidered the white muslin cradle cover with little wild-flowers and stitched a large pink and blue ribbon bow on the curved hood. 'No words can tell how I am longing to tuck my little scrap of Christopher up in its warm blankets,' she wrote in her diary.

But with motherhood added to her many duties as a Vicar's wife in a London still wincing under the siren's wail, the diary is largely forgotten. The next big event is the birth of Peter, on 16 April 1944. Then, three weeks later, D Day. 'We watch and wait,' she writes. 'One dares not dwell on the hell which these wonderful men are facing for so many of us who are so unworthy.'

But for her the ordeal was still not over. On 28 June she writes: 'For over two weeks now we have been in the line of fire without any really effective means of defence against the pilotless planes or flying bombs. They are becoming more frequent. They have already killed many of our folk and fear is creeping back into our hearts. Our nerves are never really rested. I am sure that this continual strain makes most of us feel much older than we really are. I know that I have changed a great deal in these war years.'

On 12 August she writes: 'We all tucked in under the Morrison shelter last night. The babes were asleep, one near our heads and the other, Peter, in a cardboard box at our feet. Suddenly I was awakened by a dreadful rushing sound . . . the house seemed to tremble as if an earthquake was happening. Before I had much time to realise what was happening, I had covered the children and the explosion had taken our breath away. Christopher helped me to get the dust from my mouth and made sure that the babies were safe, then he crawled out and was gone until morning came.

'He came back to tell me that two of our friends had been killed, and that our house had missed the fly-bomb by less than forty yards. As soon as it was light I surveyed the damage to the house. The mess was indescribable. We had broken curtain poles, the front door had been thrown upstairs, and, of course, there was glass in rooms, walls and carpets. The chimney will not require cleaning now for over four feet of soot fell on to the carpet. I had to fish in the soot for my wedding portrait, and after I had rubbed off some of the dirt I found myself saying, "Well, Christopher, you didn't expect this did you?" '

Five weeks later another flying bomb exploded nearby, blowing in all the temporary windows, smashing the front door again, and bringing down more ceilings. 'Such is life!' writes Joan Veazey. 'What is the good of a diary when it will probably never be read and will possibly be torn by explosions and soaked in blood?'

But the diary safely ends with the dropping of the atom bomb on Hiroshima and VJ Day, and a last entry that no doubt Joan Veazey hoped might one day be read: 'It has been wonderful to watch the end of the war. And now that we have peace, there will be no more fears of bombs and fires. As soon as we can get our men home there will be wonderful joy for many families as they are reunited. Some loved ones will never return. In honour of these men I pray that one day the world will forget its selfishness and greed, then perhaps they will not have died in vain.

'As long as we go on making new and more deadly weapons of war and destruction we shall be tempted to use them. It is for the scientists to use their brains for making healing instruments. If they do not do this . . . then the mothers of England will again cry out, "God help our children".'

8 *Diary of a Somerset Housewife*

Home Front activities in the English countryside had a diversity unknown to city-dwellers, and the diaries kept by Mrs Anne Lee-Michell, a young Somerset housewife, have a warmth and glow about them that suggest there was rarely a dull moment.

'From blitz to feeding the fowls' is her own summing-up, which does less than justice to the daily entries, between 1941 and 1945, that fill three volumes of Charles Letts' Popular Diary. A mother of two and the wife of a solicitor, her activities during the period included welfare work among evacuees, operating mobile canteens in blitz-torn Plymouth and Exeter, testing ampules in an Air Ministry water-purifying plant, and (while awaiting a medical verdict on suspected cancer) helping with the WVS during the flying-bomb assault on London.

There is a relish, even a gaiety, in many of her entries which, in retrospect, she is not so sure was not a bit forced.

'My diaries were chiefly written late at night and, on looking back through them, I wonder how and why I sat up writing. It must have been in some way a release from tension, and perhaps I felt dimly that we were assisting, however remotely, in historic events. Many entries now seem to me facetious. I think we craved humour during our anxieties and that I recorded anything that made us laugh—and there was nearly always *something*.'

Anne Garnett was born in London, in 1908, into a distinguished literary family (her uncle was Edward Garnett). She married 'Mike' Lee-Michell in 1930.

'We settled into a house we built on the outskirts of Wellington, Somerset, in fields then unspoilt. Our house had four bedrooms and stood in half an acre of meadow, which we happily made into a garden, adding a garage and tennis-court. Our first child, Sarah, was born in 1933. The next year "Mike" suddenly developed diabetes, which inevitably altered our lives. "Toots" was born in 1936, and then Munich showed us that once again everything would be different. I remember feeling thankful that we had some breathing space. I detested the idea of war and all its manifestations so much that the next months were spent in a kind of mental wrestling match.

'When war broke out the population of Wellington grew from about 7,000 to over 8,000 with the arrival of evacuees. Our house was filled with them through 1940 and 1941 and I was much occupied with billeting. Our "Beatrice", who lived in, had come to us in 1931 and was a great prop, taking cooking, washing, babies, the war and evacuees with (sometimes grim) phlegm.

'Till 1934 I had had the most untroubled life, enjoying books, riding, tennis, swimming and the country—heaven to be living in Somerset! I had absolutely no social sense, detested authority, and preferred books and animals to people. Things were indeed to be different . . .'

1941

'*2 January.* A glittering white frost. Drove the fourteen miles to Tatton Hall in the Quantock Hills, which now houses a maternity wing for evacuees, and took a mother and new baby to a condemned cottage in the wilds, up miles of snowy lanes. No cot for the baby though neighbours had lit a fire. I rang the RDC on my return, but they cannot supply a cot because the mother is still on the Urban list! It is freezing hard tonight, the bath water won't run away, dozens of Germans fly overhead, and Sarah has been sick all over her bed.

'*19 January*. At 7.30 pm to Taunton for all-night duty at the Church Army Canteen (Forces only) at the railway station. We poached eggs and washed up ceaselessly till 12.30, when a brief lull enabled us to sit down. A diversion was caused by the three-month-old baby of one of the Tatton Hall mothers. She and her nice sailor-husband had been to Scotland for his leave and were returning to Devonport. They were both tired out, so we put them to bed on four chairs and took charge of the baby; many bottles, nappy-changes etc occupied the night. Mercifully the CA Capt did not come in—*no* civilians are to be served!

'*7 March*. A large meeting re blood-giving. Lulu G., our WVS chief, was in the chair. The West of England is to give 200 pints a week, and I am to go from door to door in Mantle Street asking for pints. Hateful task!

'*2 April*. A War Comforts meeting was a solemn affair, everyone in awe of the Chairman. Lulu appealed to us to sew badges on to the Durhams' tunics, they are going to Egypt soon. So I went to the Red X depot to do this. A b—— awful job — takes ages. But chief event of the day has been the arrival of twelve hens, all starving and thirsty, and we've no food for them. Can get no sense from the Food Office who appear to have given us the wrong form; the shop refuses to sell us anything but grit. It's a pouring wet day and the hens are very dejected, however one has laid an egg. They are in a run at the garden of Bobbie's works, he and Babs are to feed them one week and Mike and I the next, sharing the eggs. Bobbie has long been feeling that the rather derelict grounds should be put to some use.

'*3 May*. The children and I cycled to pick primroses, a glorious spring day. Coming home Babs ran out of the local to say she and I had to go to Plymouth to drive the Queen's Messenger Food Convoy. Apparently the blitz there had been frightful. Rushed home to put up necessary things and drove to Plymouth with Babs, Mrs L. and Mrs W. We found a fine fleet of vans on a blitzed sports-ground—a bus upside down on top of the grandstand! I drove a van to the comparative safety of Tavistock, where the convoy spends the night. Started well but could not get into bottom gear at one point, thus stopping the whole convoy. A kind soldier on the kerb sprang in beside me: "You want to do it like *this,* Miss," and I got the hang of it. We had dinner in a pub at Tavistock and then a moonlight drive to friends of Mrs W's, who are putting us up for the three nights. Sad to see the long trails of tired folk plodding out of Plymouth.

'*4 May.* Up at cock-crow owing to the start of double summer-time, and had a very hard day's work making soup in the boilers, cutting b. and b. etc. Whole affair rather a muddle—no organisation as yet.

'*5 May.* The drive over Dartmoor is so lovely in the dawn! Such a hard day's work, we never sat down. I was sent out with a canteen through frightful rubble and desolation. Soldiers doing demolition work were thankful for tea, the dust was choking. I couldn't have imagined such scenes, whole streets nothing but twisted girders and rubble. The people were pathetic, especially the children. As Plymouth is a naval base they were not evacuated.

'*6 May.* A stray incendiary from last night's raid lit a sulky dixie very nicely! Another long day; I was glad to come off duty, dirty from the smoke of dixies.

'*1 June.* The most perfect weather—mist clearing to hot sunshine. Mike had a HG parade and the children and I went to see them stepping out with a band playing. Rather pathetic—some so elderly. They marched to church, where Mike resented the Vicar preaching about the wrong HG—Holy Ghost, it being Whit Sunday! Afternoon hanging tennis nets and marking the court—happy thoughts of tennis rudely disturbed by frightful news that we are evacuating Crete and that clothes are to be rationed.

'5 *October*. We have now added 2 young goats and a Nanny to our fowls and ducks. Bobbie enthusiastic about this, and I had a nightmare the other night in which he had bought a camel—"No trouble, and so useful with petrol short". Mike and Babs do not share his zeal, so he and I are to milk. Babs phoned to say she thinks Miranda is in season, and that the sick pullet is dead. Nanny too was duly served by the willing Miguel, we then used precious petrol to drive to the inn where the landlord sold her as "in kid". He offered to exchange her for a dismal old goat still giving a pint of milk a day. Awful query: could we milk her? Bobbie and I tried, to no avail, and are to go each pm till we succeed.

'25 *November*. The usual milking and agriculture led to an eventful day. I got two helpers for the evacuee clinic, of which I now appear to be in charge; we were busy weighing babies and advising the mothers of the most sickly *not* to put them on Full Cream Milk! Hurried back to milk and put goats, hens and ducks to bed and change for Report Centre Duty. We are now paid 9d an hour! I had barely settled down with my knitting when a "Purple Warning" came through. As I am the telephonist I sprang to the phone, only to be stopped by old Baxter, who said "Do nothing till we are sure." The siren went and wardens trooped in; machine guns rattled overhead and then came 2 terrific crumps. Reports came in thick and fast, but still Baxter wouldn't let me phone! The bombs had fallen at Payton, about 1½ miles off. Came away for polite bridge at Mrs Bell's. Home at midnight to find Mike very muddy, having fallen into a bomb crater while searching for a plane reported crashed.

'5 *December*. Arranging the WVS office for a shop for "Mrs Churchill's Aid to Russia Fund". Goods flowed in—I tried to flog a Raphael print to an evacuee but she said "I'm not much of a one for the Virgin"!

'The day ended with the Home Guard dance—500 HGs milling over my feet! When I went to milk next am Bab's Ivy said "Poor mistress is upstairs bathing her feet. I'm sorry there's no aspirin, but she has two vegetarians on her bed"! Dear Ivy, how she brightens our war.'

1942

'*9 January*. We have had a letter from the LCC about a damsel, Phyllis O'Reilly, being evacuated to us "in need of care". In veiled language they infer that her mother sends her on the streets. At the clinic a note from said mother asked for baby-food —she has just had her 9th—which she couldn't fetch as she has gone to London to bring Phyllis. Another baby is desperately ill, the doctor says the mother *must* leave their condemned cottage. What can one do? No one is allowed to help these women who have come down on their own initiative.

'We have had a continuous rush at the Church Army Canteen, which was even more sordid and filthy than usual. As it never closes it can never be thoroughly cleaned, though we do our best during brief lulls. A soldier said it was girls like us who were winning the war, and gave me 2d!

'*13 January*. Lively stories about Phyllis O'Reilly. A startlingly pretty girl, she promptly took a job here with the (to her) most suitable employer, a noted lecher. Babs gave a lift to one of the nuns in charge of the evacuated East End School, who stoutly defended Mrs O'Reilly, saying she is a wonderful mother to her nine offspring (all by different fathers). Sister Malone attributes the O'R. morals entirely to the "dark alcoves" in their late tenement. She appears to feel alcoves incompatible with purity.

'*10 February*. We hear that the father of the latest O'Reilly baby has arrived in Wellington, and is living sinfully with Mrs O'R. in her billet, to the great scandalisation of the landlady. He is a boxer, 6 ft 4 inches high, and threatens violence when told to leave—landlord being only 5 ft 8 inches. The police, when appealed to, say that "nothing can be done till an assault has been committed".

'*24 February*. Attended a large meeting of wardens and housewives, the idea being that the two are to combine in the event of a blitz. But sad to say the wardens appear to dislike us intensely—all very difficult! The meeting dragged on till 9.15 when it broke up in disorder. Home to supper (small portion of bony whiting) and stacks of mending.

'2 *March.* A truly noble dinner of a deceased fowl—we tossed for it yesterday and Jean won. She and Don now share our labours (and assets) with the fowls, but not the goats. Came home by bright moonlight clutching two white counterpanes she has thrown out, the fowl's wishbone and parson's nose, and the best part of a bottle of hock for Mike, who is in bed with what appears to be flu.

'7 *March.* Great event of the week—Miranda has dropped a fine kid! It is a billy, so is to be fattened for the table.

'11 *March.* Mike is really ill, it's been a day of intensive nursing, weighing grammes of sugar, doing tests and rinsing insulin syringes. Apart from the anxiety of it being Mike, it's rather fascinating nursing a diabetic. In between this I dashed to and fro to the animals—Miranda has been yelling her head off since the kid's birth, but it is fine.

'25 *March.* In the afternoon there was a MOI film at the cinema and a rather dull harangue from St John Ervine. He and his wife had tea with us, we were asked to have them on the strength of his having mentioned Aunt Constance Garnett in a recent broadcast. He told me a good story of Uncle Edward Garnett. A man was always bragging about the fact that he lived with two fishermen, wore a fisherman's jersey and made rather an exhibition of himself at a literary club E. frequented. One day E. said "Oh, you live with two fishermen, don't you?" "Yes, yes . . ." "One day you are going to meet a man who lives with three fishermen, and what will you do then?"

'12 *April.* Feeding 6,000 munition workers at Weston-super-Mare with the WVS canteen. They lined the sea-wall watching the Army demonstrate just how well their munitions worked. There was a ceaseless racket of machine-guns, bombs and large guns which broke windows all down the parade.

'In the afternoon I had to take our kid to the butcher's on a lead, and stayed hiding in a hedge while the children passed by, afraid of upsetting them. I left it in the slaughter-house with a heavy heart.

'*5 May.* A long procession of weary firemen returning from Exeter. It was burning all last night. One told me that things are terrible there—we'll have our work cut out tomorrow. I had to set out to Apley Cross school with tins of food from the communal kitchen, and one came open and deposited stew all over the back seat of the car. Ate my dinner with the twenty-three London and Bristol children there, and they helped me clear up the mess. Then went round delivering USA Red X satchels to everyone going to Exeter, sent us for such a purpose and languishing in store ever since.

'*6 May.* Twenty-six of us off to Exeter by the early train, which waited a long time outside the city while men repaired the line. The vans were parked in Bury Meadow and we took over from the Taunton team and in no time at all were flat out cutting sandwiches and serving teas to an endless queue of people. It was fearfully hot and we dripped with sweat. Then I was sent out in a van. Exeter was fantastic—the High St just a narrow track between shattered walls and piles of debris, choking white dust, and sweating soldiers clearing a wider path.

'Our affairs were much better organised than at Plymouth, we had a good sit-down at a hotel, and didn't have to look after fires and dixies—soldiers and ARP did them, and carried the heavy urns for us. About 8 pm we loaded up and drove out to Chudleigh—heavenly drive through woods sheeted with primroses—to an immense Georgian mansion set in a park. Girl Guides whom I remembered at Plymouth had a good hot supper for us and then all we asked was a BED.

'*7 May.* Alas, we had the worst night of our lives, tossing on thin palliasses on the library floor, me with my head under a sofa and my feet on a Chinese idol! So we all started tired and jaded, and there was a ridiculous fuss because I wanted the milk scalded (it went sour yesterday) and the Min of Food man stood the churns in the dixies for me without consulting the WVS boss. She was furious—especially when it worked and the milk remained sweet.

'Toiled all day and went out twice—great amusement when a soldier said "You ain't stopped in a very good place, Miss" and I looked up and saw a wall tottering in a slant above us! Babs was asked by a policeman to feed some men digging up an unexploded bomb. She asked them when it would go off—"Oh, about now, Miss." "Now then boys—drink up—we must be off!" called Mrs Hill from the back! Actually got a bed tonight and slept like a log. Am amazed at "filthy-dirty" pictures adorning the bathrooms and lavs in this sumptious abode.

'*8 May.* Our last day here, we came off duty at lunch and strolled about the ruins. The King and Queen were doing the same thing in company with the Mayor, and our train had to await the departure of the royal one. We stood, incredibly filthy and tired, on the platform waiting and got a kindly smile from their Majesties. The King indeed almost laughed when he caught sight of Babs perched on some steps, a huge smut all down her face, but bowing and smiling in a truly regal manner. She is extraordinarily like the Queen and must have seemed a sooty caricature!

'Our train when it came, crawled along, packed with evacuees and was very late. Bobbie and Mike had come to meet us and gone on to an HG conference. But we got home—and how green and flowery the garden, and pink and clean the children tucked up in bed!

'*9 June.* We are now collecting and drying nettles and foxgloves (the former makes chlorophyll, the latter for digitalis), also sphagnum moss which is terribly heavy to carry in sacks and full of black slugs! It will be used as deodorant dressings for gangrene etc. There were two enormous sacks of nettles dumped at the WVS office today, one alas full of weeds and grass. I fetched mothers and babies from a distant village to the clinic, so many evacuees have left that doctor and nurse grumble at coming to attend so few. "I don't know why you complain," said Babs absently. "You get paid, we do it for nothing." Doctor and nurse quite stunned by this! Little Rita has worms *again,* and will evermore I fear, as the doctor says a daily enema is the only cure, and Nurse won't go unless Mum pays 2s or an 8s sub, which Mum says she can't afford. Deadlock—meanwhile Rita's worms writhe within and all is corruption . . .

'*14 June.* We filled the canteen up and I drove it to the Recreation Ground, returning to take my place in a long procession—HG, Soldiers, OTC, Guides, Scouts and ourselves, behind with the dust-cart as usual. At the last moment a gent bearing a banner emblazoned "Your Sins are Scarlet, Wash them in the Blood of the Lamb" inserted himself just in front of Lulu, who had to march stoutly along none the less!

'The whole affair was in honour of "United Nations Day". We marched to the ground trying to keep in step—difficult, as we were just far enough from both bands to hear different rhythms. We then stood to attention being harangued, and there was a prayer beginning "O Almighty God who has created all men of one blood to be brothers" and ending "Help us to give the Germans Hell" or words to that effect.

'*10 July.* The children's headmistress says that her junior teacher is being called up, so all the elder children must leave. A fearful blow—we shall have to find a boarding school for Sarah, and how can we afford that? However Don offers me a part-time job at his factory, which is a place of mystery but apparently they make water-purifying plant for the Air Ministry. Feel I ought to accept as it would just about pay for Sarah's school (£2 a week).

'*8 August.* On going to milk yesterday I met a large negro, directing the traffic; a party of black Pioneers have now arrived to dig a hole in the road, watched mournfully by our Town Surveyor and Manager of the Gasworks. The camp is to be in a large field behind Bobbie and Babs (and our farm)—a lovely meadow that produces tons of hay. I take this hard after a Min of Ag broadcast urging us to use "every square inch" for food! I spent the evening making gym shorts for Sarah out of the dress I had for my 21st birthday, once green but long since dyed black and converted into a long skirt. It was the nicest dress I ever had and I'm pleased it has an honourable end.

'*9 August*. Babs' small Jeremy came weeping—"The black peoples have come to take me away", but later made friends and was given 1½d by a Sambo—America's first personal gift to Wellington.

'*12 August*. Wellington is a seething mass of darkies now, followed by children, who can't leave them alone. There is a forest of tents in the meadow—nice for Bobbie and Babs, who are awakened at 5 am by chattering, laughter and blowing of whistles. Our local girls are much attracted and Bobbie's foreman saw three at the camp gate, looking longingly in. "They maids—prick-mazed they be, prick-mazed" was his comment.

'To the cinema this evening to collect for St Dunstan's. There was a short film on the blind, then the lights went up and round we went with our tins and the ghastly collector's smile pinned to our faces. The negroes gave lavishly; their opinion of England is "a place where there is hardly any food and no money"! Our Beatrice and Ivy went to the pictures together recently, and Ivy reported "A lovely film, all about Tarzan in the Junction. And the short one was ever so nice, about two girls, and the dark one wanted to be as pretty as the fair one, so she went to the hairdresser and came out a *blange*". Ivy is nearly as refreshing as "Itma".

'*8 September*. First day at work. Cycled the three miles, and picked my way through rubble and derelict sheds of a disused textile mill. At length found a notice "Keep out", so went in and enquired for Don. My dept is a small office off the glass-blowing bay, and I am to inspect glass ampules containing chlorus, with a cheerful Cockney, George. I found it difficult to see minute cracks and bubbles in the sealing, and my eyes grew sore holding the racks of ampules against a bright strip light. Came home weary to a late supper and a most cheering speech from Churchill. Can't think what we'd do without him.

'*1 October.* A letter from Aunt Olive Garnett, who is appalled at the idea of "Books by the Mile for Salvage". Not a notion to appeal to any Garnett; I should think Grandpa Richard's grave in Highgate Cemetery is turning nicely.

'*13 October.* On returning from Report duty I was electrified to find an enormous Negro sprawling in the kitchen arm-chair, our Beatrice perched on his knee. When she brought our supper she offered us a glass of his beer, which we thankfully accepted. I was telling her of my difficulties in getting home through posses of too-gallant Yanks and she replied "Now you know what we girls have to put up with"! We heard later that her "Coloured Friend" had called at our local, and on being asked who his girl-friend was, swallowed 2 whiskies and replied "I'm just off to try my luck"!

'*16 December.* A radiant Sarah home from school, and Toots keeps feeling her to make sure. I keep thinking of one Geraldine who cried last night. "You see, Mummy, she has no real home—she has to go to her Granny." Alas, so many now have no real home. Intensive half-hour helping the children with their Xmas cards—"How do you spell Rosemary?" "My pen won't write." "Be quiet, Toots", etc etc. Also Xmas shopping with them—difficult as they mutter under their breath and only tweak my elbow in agony after I've bought the wrong thing.

'*31 December.* Thank God we have better news than this time last year, when every day brought fresh disaster. Now we've chased Rommel nearly to Tripoli and the Russians are steadily pushing the Germans back. A lovely party at the officers' Mess, for which we laid a basis at the local. All the officers were in grand form, we played darts, sang and danced and brought the New Year in with much ceremony. The Colonel grew a bit tight; clasped Babs to his bosom while dancing and murmured into her hair "I'm a passionate man—I adore brunettes"! The only sad notes were Helen's and D's faces—H's husband has just gone over-seas and D's was killed at Alamein. Bobbie took her home early when she whispered "I can't stand any more".'

1943

'*24 January.* A large exercise in Taunton, to which Babs and I took the canteen. The town was swept and garnished for the fray, empty streets adorned with little knots of earnest, tin-hatted wardens and police, fire-engines at the ready. We were sent from pillar to post; amusing scenes as incendiaries were let off. In a pitch-black cellar a face peered at us through a grill, the cellar was then "blown up", and its occupants carried out on stretchers. Out to a school in the afternoon to feed some lone women, swarms of little boys made themselves obnoxious and the most odious (the Headmaster's son) soused me in scalding tea. Home at last, very weary, just as Bobbie came in having been an Umpire all day. The general opinion is that the exercise went well.

'*25 February.* We now have an allotment! Quite a large one and I confess I echo Toots' sigh as she dug her little garden recently: "I wish I hadn't so much land"! Today I trundled loads of goat-manure on to it, and double-trenched—so easy in the diagrams in gardening books, such hell in reality, as the top-spit caves over and falls into one's boots. Toots hove in sight, pleased to see me as she'd been home to an empty house. "Did you cry?"I asked, and she said "Yes, but I asked God where you were and he told me." She is full of philosophy and the other day said "I shall always be happy." "How will you manage that?" we asked. "Oh, I shall always love *everyone*." We met Babs, still laughing at Ivy who is indignant at the "dolts" having extra rations. It seems she heard a broadcast about certain classes of adult workers.

'*18 May.* Every type of fighter and bomber flew over us last night, some so low they seemed to skim the roof. At 3.30 the siren wailed and battles raged overhead. There was a loud burst of machine-guns, then a blinding flash and the most tremendous explosion. The house fairly reeled—then another. We rushed to the nursery. Toots had disappeared and we feared she'd been sucked out of the window. However, she was at the bottom of her bed, shaking with fright. We trekked down to the air-raid shelter and were quite snug with rugs, cushions and the electric fire. Mike got into his HG regalia and prowled around while planes shrieked by, bombs fell and guns muttered. All clear at 4.30.

'*19 May.* We hear the crumps last night were caused by two land-mines falling at Nowers—the dear old house is completely ruined though Mrs P. and her housekeeper survive.

'*20 May.* Nowers is pathetic—broken glass everywhere, even in tightly-closed drawers and tins in the larder. All the lovely things in the house destroyed, but by some uncanny Power dying stags and Pampas grass survive.

'*13 July.* Since 2.30 am a continuous stream of bombers have been straggling home, one, as our postman said, "Fair crippled". Alarming tale from a farmer in the local of an Italian prisoner who ran amok, cut off his guard's head with a bill-hook, took a pot-shot at a Land Girl with the guard's gun, and hid in the woods. He was later found at a farm, where a brave boy of eighteen pursued him upstairs, found him with the gun levelled and shot him dead. The farmer is having twenty-five of them to pull his flax two fields away from us on Thursday!

'*28 September.* A cold north wind makes us shiver and long for winter woollies. The Board of Trade issues a moral little booklet "Make and Mend", exhorting us to cut the feet from old stockings, pick up the stitches and knit new feet, with creased turn-downs to hide the joins. Am doing this, but for other tips such as "Sew up all pleats and button-holes before putting clothes away" and "Reinforce all elbows, knees and pockets on new clothes before putting them on" I've little use and less time.

'*11 October.* I am told of a sad end to the O'Reilly Saga.

Phyllis is missing again, and Mrs O'R. went to London to find her, taking the new baby (No ten and presumably the boxer's). She found that Phyllis has been living with him but had already left, and the boxer in despair has committed suicide.

'*3 November.* A respectable matron here, followed by a negro last night, lost her nerve and broke into a run. He jumped at her and slashed her breast and neck with a knife. Her screams brought a passing cyclist (her brother-in-law) who took her off for first aid. The darkie has since been arrested, but another is missing from the camp. I hope I don't encounter him in our hay-shed when I go there in the dark! On expressing this fear to Bobbie all I got was "My dear Anne, no one could get near you in those dungarees—the smell of goat . . . !"

'*25 November.* WVS Day Training School at the Shire Hall. We sat in the Council Room and listened to enthralling lectures on blitzes. The speakers positively glowed as they outlined horrors to come—quite sure we'd have more blitzes, and even more hopefully, gas attacks!

'*27 November.* Making successful crackers from coloured paper and HG "cracker-blanks"—left over from an exercise—"a Top-Guarded-Secret", Mike says! Toots, admonishing her dolls: "No, you won't see Father Xmas this year, so it's no use making a fuss. He's been called up, so there's an end to it"!

'*18 December.* Hectic preparations for Xmas party at the Works, for which twelve black-market geese have been roasting in the huge ovens. Spent the morning standing on ladders, transforming our bay into a tropical scene with South Sea Island girls, parrots and monkeys designed and executed by me. Old Smith disapproves of my Island beauties—titties the wrong colour, he says! Met my Mother and aunt, who have come for Xmas, and prepared their supper as Beatrice is helping at the party, then Mike and I set out for the works.

'Whole place transformed—fairy lights everywhere, and the glass-shop an Aladdin's Cave with thousands of paper streamers and lacy cut-outs fluttering from the roof. Masses of drinks in

Don's office where a select band had gathered. The dinner went well, Beatrice and some chums of hers darting round with plates of soup, goose and mince-pies; beer flowed.

'We then trooped up to our bay, whose tropical splendours were dimmed by the stage lights fusing. Lavish presents off the tree and then more drinks and highly successful dancing in the painting-bay. I have dim memories of kissing a director and being told that our bay had won the 1st prize—100 cigarettes!

'*24 December.* After washing-up at the works, the afternoon saw the family on the road with a huge basket of gifts, trudging wearily round with pots of bulbs, holly, silver leaves etc for friends and evacuees. Returned even more weighted with flour, bread and a large joint (rations for seven) the butcher insisted on my taking. Decorated the house with the children and then out after supper to deliver more presents, drinks everywhere and even I felt I'd never look a gin and french in the eye again! Home at midnight to fill stockings and tip-toe about with parcels.'

1944

'*29 March.* Hilarity over a billeting form served on us today (our schoolmaster lodger left some time ago as his school moved). "You are required to billet 1 officer, 3s per day, horses 3s 9d per day, and to give each horse 5 lb oats, 10 lb hay, officers 10 oz of meat, 1 oz butter, 10 oz vegetables for dinner" etc etc, and ending "the manure remains the property of the War Office".

'To bed early for once, to be aroused by the siren at 11.30. Turned wearily out with sweater and trousers over my pyjamas, to join shrouded group of Fire Guards outside our local. Was made to put on my tin hat as machine-gunning was heard. At last I sat miserably down on my tin hat, and a figure loomed up and told me how actresses keep their tights up! Up early after this and off in a hired car to meet the children for their holidays. Our soldier-guest has appeared, a young fair-haired Texan. He is thrilled with home comforts and a large bed, his first for two years.

'*3 April.* One of our tanks in the roof is leaking and water drips on to the landing. Bill the Texan commented: "Not so hot for the shack"! Very tired to-night—did 3,000 ampules at the works. We had a grand pep talk from Don—big new contracts, anyone who doesn't like it can quit, etc. So stirred by this I offered to do more hours—"Don't be silly, Anne, it was only a pep-talk"!

'I think old Mabel's kid is due, she is so heavy and apathetic. She really is the dreariest creature, apart from self! While doing the farming a USA jeep drew up, full of officers and Babs in her best dress among them, clutching three carnations! She'd been asked to be matron of honour at a wedding in Taunton. They held a party at the local to celebrate, and the evening ended in someone's house with inebriated guests and a band. Our Texan Bill consumed much neat whisky, and whisked us around; when we got home at 12.30 he insisted on playing Black-jack.

'*14 April.* I have it on old Smith's authority that the second front will start tomorrow. They certainly must have nearly enough stuff, I can hardly cycle to work for troops, guns, boats, lorries etc in never-ending streams down the main road. Sat up late talking to Bill. He doesn't talk so much as "hold forth", and told me of his mother, who drank to excess: "A fine little lady, Ma'am, I'm proud of her . . ."!

'*18 April.* Bill announced to Beatrice that he was going to get drunk, whereupon she replied "You were drunk the other night, weren't you?" He admitted "Well, I did kinda fall over my feet coming up the stairs." He sleeps heavily and Beatrice takes it on herself to shake him awake in time for parade. "It's plenty tough to open your eyes on that old witch"! He brought us masses of sweets and cigarettes today.

'*25 April.* We had a great riding picnic today. Our two and Jane went with the riding-school mistress on ponies and I and the little girls on bikes with the tea. No sooner were we on a steep path through the woods than the Yanks began firing in the butts below, and bullets came pinging unpleasantly close. Bark flew off trees by us and we had to crawl on our stomachs. The girls loved it but it gave me a very cold sensation when a shot pinged past. The pony contingent cantered up safely and we tethered the ponies behind a high earthen bank where they kicked and plunged. We lay flat to eat our tea, endeavouring to keep the young prone. Half way through I realised I'd left our precious big thermos in the wood, and with beating heart crawled down to fetch it. We returned home by a safer route. Joys of war-time!

'*10 May*. Every night now dozens of huge transport planes go roaring round and round, a lovely sight with their red and green lights, especially as they turn and you see both red and green at once in a long jewelled train. It's hard to tell stars from planes now, the sky is so full of both, and the great steady swords of searchlights. This lovely weather certainly helps us bear the suspense. Bill is leaving us to live in camp.

'*6 June*. Mike called me in from a pre-breakfast prowl in the dewy garden: "I think the Second Front has started." We thought it might, last night the planes flew off as usual but did not return . . . Sick with excitement all day, hoping and praying . . .

'*9 June*. Very wan breakfast after discovery of a sinister knob in my left breast. Cycled to the doc who takes a poor view and says I *must* see a specialist. Broke the news to Don who puts me on sick-leave. Touching farewells at the works and good wishes. Hurried about winding up WVS jobs etc. In the local at lunch-time were two glider-pilots, full of their grim experiences landing in France. Only eight returned, out of "more than forty". One was cheery and tough, the other had glassy, gooseberry eyes full of horror. We went to see "Claudia" after supper, an amusing film but we laughed most when the Mother turned out to have incurable cancer!

'*12 June*. To town to see Jimmy the specialist. A clean, bright empty London of wide streets and green rustling trees. How beautiful it is when one can see it! A noisy night with sirens wailing. Jimmy charming and reassuring, but no beds to be had as all the hospitals are kept clear for casualties. I must just wait.

'*12 July*. Hailed from lunch by an urgent summons to London. Mrs L. is going up for WVS duty and can't get a soul to go with her. Packed and got a lift to Taunton, met Mrs L. and had a pleasant journey in empty train—London not popular just now! "Raid On" placards greeted us, however the All Clear went quite soon. We are billeted with eighty-five WVS at the Duchess Club for Officers behind the BBC. Whole affair reminiscent of school—women formidable, women shy, rush on baths and lavs, excited groups being briefed. Am to do "clothing" and then "Urns and ashes"—sounds funereal. The night-porter has just been in to put up my black-out. Sat on my bed and told me *a.* he deals in whisky, *b.* has nine children, and *c.* is a Passionate Man.

'*14 July*. Am briefed to do office work in Tothill St. Rang Jimmy who said sadly "No bed yet" but he would like to see me at 4.30 at the Middlesex. Got off duty to go to the Middlesex and fell fast asleep on a soft couch. Woken by Jimmy who, joy of joys, offered me a bed on Monday! My spirits rose and I floated out and into All Saints, Margaret St (where I was confirmed) for some of the evening plainsong. Lovely evening with old friends at Eaton Place.

'*17 July*. Very noisy night with Doodles and women stampeding to lower quarters . . . We were station-marshalls at St Pancras today. One evacuee child was mysteriously lost, the water and biscuits were late in arriving, and I had to keep phoning from the station-master's office about them. As I raced down the train with a precious spoon for the babies' feeds (stolen from the restaurant and I was pursued by irate staff—"You WVS take all our spoons")—the elastic in my pants broke and they descended! Loud cheers from all beholders as I took them off and waved them to the departing train.

'Just as we had seventy children assembled a Doodle chose to cut out just above the glass roof. I got them down under a stack of mail-bags and prayed hard. It went on, and came down I heard later in Regents Park. After this I went out and bought £2-worth of books and taxied to hospital, where it's been bliss to be bathed and have my blisters pricked by kind nurses, and be put into a spotless bed.

'*19 July*. Two days of perfect rest. Mike has been up to see me and has fallen for the lovely Australian blonde next me, in for a miscarriage. She and her two babies are stranded in London so we've urged them to come to us now Bill is overseas.

'I was cleansed and purged this morning and awoke at 2 feeling exactly like a Paschal lamb, to be told by a beaming nurse that the frozen section was negative, and that all that has to be done is the removal of the cyst. Heavenly gratitude and bliss—and best of all was Mike's face when he came to see me. Sound sleep between the crumps of doodles and I feel I've never known before what peace is.'

But life back at Wellington continued as hectically and unpredictably as before. For three months, after her Pilot Officer husband had been recalled to duty in Australia, the 'lovely Australian blonde' and her two little tomboy daughters occupied the spare room ('occupied in '41 by four evacuees, and two under the dining table'). She proved a kindred spirit ('she shares all our pleasures and is great at skittles') and Mrs Lee-Michell saw them off 'with a lump in my throat—we shall miss them terribly'. A day in January 1945 marked an even sadder occasion. 'Our dear Beatrice has had to leave us to tend her aged mother. The awful sound of her corded bales departing has filled the house. I have had to leave the works, and resign from divers jobs.'

The war was moving to a close. She drove the WVS canteen for the last time—to Bristol, to be handed over for service in Belgium. At the end of the Easter holidays, she consoled herself for the departure of Sarah and Toots, both now at boarding-school, by going to see an old friend just back from Burma ('It's wonderful to be welcoming men back instead of seeing them off'). One of the GIs they had wished God-speed to a year before dropped in at the local one night, a lieutenant-colonel now. 'Nice to see him, and hear that they are all safe, though he was wounded in the throat twice. No news of Texan Bill, who has left the Company.'

The busy, gossipy, harassed, hilarious, diary entries reach their culmination—VE Day and VJ Day . . .

'*8 May*. Glorious day! Sunshine, flags and happy crowds, and the marvellous feeling of relief. We made holiday all day, ending with a terrific party next door. Came home tonight—a bonfire and dancing round it. Mike and I went to church at 7.30 pm, there was an immense congregation with people standing.'

'*14 August*. I came down to hear the long-awaited news. Up went our flags, and we bustled through our work. A great Victory Dinner, one of our three old ducks, green peas, and chocolate pears. In the evening a vast bonfire at Hilly Head, and back here for a firework party.

'But in spite of the joy one can't help reflecting that our larders are bare, there are no houses for our returning soldiers, and that some sea-change has affected even the wonderful Churchill! Everyone's house needs painting and replastering, our clothes are shabby, and one can't buy a sheet or a blanket unless one is bombed-out or newly wed. Among the blessings promised are the nationalisation of coal, electricity and the Board of Education! Life is going to be every bit as strenuous; we are all exhausted . . . The best minute of the day has been just to sit down and realise that the war is over.'

9 *Buzz Bomb Summer*

Seen through the eyes of a child, an air raid could have an element of exhilaration as much as fear. Taking for granted the everyday restrictions and privations of life on the Home Front that so preoccupied his elders, he looked for something out of the ordinary to make war meaningful. And war came to his very doorstep with the wail of the sirens, the dash to the shelter, every sense alert to that throb of menace in the sky.

It is this sense of wide-eyed excitement that comes over most strongly in 'Buzz Bomb Summer' by Lionel King, an account of the V1 onslaught on London based on the diaries he kept at the time, at the age of eight. For over three weeks, before being evacuated, he noted down each occasion when one of Hitler's 'secret weapons' growled and spluttered overhead, or suddenly stopped and plunged.

The V1s—successively known as flying bombs, pilotless planes, buzz bombs and doodlebugs—are briefly disposed of in most war histories. First launched on 12 June 1944, in a desperate new bid to shatter civilian morale, they had killed 5,475, seriously injured 16,000, and wrecked 25,000 houses in the London area by the end of September, when their launching sites had mostly been over-run by the Allied armies. At the height of this indiscriminate bombardment, they were coming over in a day-and-night procession, sometimes up to nine visible in the sky at one time, and air raid warnings were abandoned. During the period nearly a million and a half Londoners were evacuated. Evelyn Waugh summed up the feelings of fear and revulsion: 'It was as impersonal as a plague, as though the city were infested with enormous, venomous insects.'

To young Lionel King, already experienced in 'conventional' air raids, it was something entirely novel. Buzz-bomb-spotting became a new challenge among friends. But sometimes an engine cut, and there were terrible things to note down. The corner shops in Thornhill Road were just a heap of rubble. Jimmy Ward's jolly mother hadn't bothered to sleep in the shelter and was buried alive. It all goes down in the diary, a clear-cut picture of a family and a neighbourhood once again phlegmatically 'taking it'.

Lionel King was living in Grange Park Road, Leyton, E10, with his parents, his six-year-old brother Douglas, and his grandmother ('Nanny'). His father, a machine operator, had been a regular soldier but was exempted from service in order to train the Home Guard, in which he was a sergeant. His Aunt Joyce, who normally lived with them, was serving with the ATS.

King had kept a diary since he first learnt to write, at seven, and continued to do so until he was twelve. During his last year in grammar school he began to write a teenage autobiography, to be called 'Eighteen', making copious use of his boyhood diaries, only altering grammar and punctuation and inserting 'afterthoughts'.

It was from this manuscript, dug out from his loft, that King extracted 'Buzz Bomb Summer' after reading of the *Sunday Times*' interest in war memoirs. 'I abandoned the autobiography when my adolescent dream of literary fame evaporated,' he writes. 'The original diaries I destroyed in a purge of possessions prior to going to University in 1955. But this extract is basically what I noted down at the age of eight. I am delighted—and a little surprised—that it should prove of interest. Come to think of it, a lot of stuff scribbled in the war must be lying around because people are shy of showing it. Much history must be lost that way.'

'Buzz Bomb Summer' starts on 6 June 1944.

' "D Day has come!" exclaimed my mother one sunny afternoon as I came in from school. "They're saying prayers over at the Church this evening."

'While we were having games at school that morning, we had all looked up to see a glider being towed along through the sky. I had thought something was going on. There had been rumours that lots of soldiers had been sleeping in tents up at Whipps Cross and then moving away next morning. One afternoon a long procession of tanks, tiny ones, had passed through the street. Everyone was laughing at one which had NO LEAVE NO BABIES chalked on the side. I had wondered why.

'My father came in from work at 6 o'clock. He listened to the news and then took out a special *Daily Telegraph* map and pencilled in the landing beaches on the Normandy coast. He was all very enthusiastic. On my Collins Atlas I had been busily plotting the Allied advance up the Italian peninsula. Geography was my best subject.

'On the night of 12 June the first of Hitler's V1s fell on London and the South East. News spread in from the Kent and Sussex coasts of aircraft with "jet nozzles", "fire exhausts" and odd engine sounds. Over Kent some of these craft had suddenly stopped and fallen with a devastating explosion to follow. Bombing of course was familiar to our family. We had moved from West Ham earlier in the war. I'd spent endless nights in the dugout in the garden unable to sleep because of Nanny's snoring. Now it was happening in the day time too.

'The first came over one afternoon. Our windows and doors were open in those fine June days and the drone of the approaching flying bomb was quite unmistakable. It gave us little warning. Ten seconds and the engine cut out directly overhead. There was an oddly resounding explosion about half a mile away.

'The Boy Foot, as my mother called him, cycled up there and reported back: "King Edward Road—there's debris everywhere. Fire brigade and wardens are there, still digging 'em out. I saw it coming. I was up on the roof." I was envious of his roof. You could have seen anything from there.

' "Where's King Edward Road, Mum?" asked Doug.

' "By the County Ground. It's where Mr Gibbons lives—you know, he's in the Home Guard with Dad."

'Next day we took to the shelter when we heard the drone. Again the engine cut out, again seemingly over the house. Then it spluttered into life again. Doug and I laughed out loud. It was all rather a joke. Mum told us to duck. The droning engine had stopped. Eight seconds wait. A disappointing, unspectacular bang.

' "I'll find out where it dropped when I go up the shops in a minute," said Mum. "Don't open the door to any knocks." Later she told us it had fallen on a railway siding behind the dust destructor. Three old railway trucks were destroyed, a railwayman had told her.

'Soon so many V1s were coming over the authorities gave up air raid warnings. They would have been sounding the siren all the time. When a bomb announced its approach, Doug and I dived for the shelter, not forgetting to grab our cat Jimmy if he was in sight. Sometimes Mum was out shopping and we went to the shelter alone. We were never worried or afraid. It was all over in ten seconds anyway.

'One such afternoon a V1 fell further up the road. We jumped out of the shelter and saw a huge mushroom of dust and rubble rising above the roof tops. You could see individual bricks and planks of wood sailing up into the clear sky. It looked after a few seconds like a ragged umbrella. The traffic picked up again in the road. We ran through the house to the front door. Droves of people were rushing up the road, some on bicycles, many in great distress, towards the scene. Many we knew by sight.

' "There goes that man from the oil shop," exclaimed Doug.

We'd never seen him this side of the counter before. The dust cloud had settled now. The first ambulances were pulling up at the Rest Centre at the church opposite. Scruffy looking people, some shaking, were being helped in. Mum appeared. "Back into the house!" she barked. "Nanny will be home from work soon. She'll tell you all about it."

'Nanny came in later. The buzz bomb had fallen by her factory. "Mrs Lea has copped it. It fell on her house in Lea Hall Road. It's in a state round there. When it exploded the foreman told her she could go round and see if her place was all right. I went with her. We went through it two or three minutes after it happened . . ." The incident was not without humour for Doug and I. "A spotter on Jenkins' roof saw it coming. He just threw himself over the edge. It's eighty feet off the ground."

'Next day we rushed to the shelter again. A buzz bomb with a strangely healthy sound from it roared over. "That one's on its way," Mum commented. "That one's not going to drop." We listened to it disappear from earshot. Next day a caller told us, "Fell at Barnet, they say. That's the furthest he got yet."

'Day after day the rush to the shelter. A cut out. A distant explosion. Back to play in the garden. One breakfast Mum rushed in from the kitchen: "One coming!" From the shelter the explosion seemed close. "Fell at the Caribonum," Clifford, the boy next door, told us later. Nanny came home with news one evening: "That feller who jumped off the roof . . . he's all right. Only broke both his legs."

'Mrs Saddington was visiting us one afternoon with her horrid little Michael who was always crying and staying away from school. She lived up the road but was always going away to Watford—Leyton wasn't good enough for her. "Quick! There's one coming. Into the shelter!" Down we whisked. Mrs Saddington had not experienced the drill. She was a timid little woman who smelt of perfume. The buzz bomb arrived and spluttered out overhead. "I want my husband!" whimpered Mrs S. Doug and

I, hardened veterans, laughed. "You'll be all right, dear," Mum comforted her. The explosion was some way off. "We can get out now."

'There was a lull for a few days and no bombs appeared. Nanny took us out for a little walk one evening. All the evenings were fine. We passed the trolley bus stop outside Inspector MacMillan's house. The Boy Foot and his girl friend were sitting on the low wall, waiting for a bus. "Going to chance the pictures?" Nanny asked jauntily. They smiled assent. I was a little shocked to think anyone would risk being in a cinema. When we got back, Dad was talking to Mr Salt over the garden fence. "The V1s are being dropped on the Normandy beaches," said Mr Salt. "That's why we've had none over."

'One Saturday night we were awakened suddenly from our sleep in the shelter by the sound of glass fragmenting in a long crescendo, as if countless objects were slowly being slid off a ledge. It must have been about 1 am.

' "Oh Frank! That's our home gone!" shrieked our mother.

' "Can't get the bloody door open," Dad snarled as he lunged at it with his shoulder. "It's that wooden prop blocking it again." A warden's voice bellowed along the street, "Everyone all right?" Dad got the door open and went out.

' "Where did it drop?" we asked when he got back.

' "Thornhill Road." He sounded grim. "Go back to sleep."

'Thornhill Road! That was close—barely a hundred yards away. And next morning it was cleaning up time. All our window-panes were gone and the plaster down from the ceilings, leaving bare lathes in the centre. Dust everywhere. In Nanny's room large lumps of ceiling lay on her eiderdown. She was away visiting Auntie Joy stationed at Newmarket. "We'll clear it up before she comes back," Dad promised.

'We took a walk along to see the bomb damage. Between our house and the junction of Grange Park Road with the High Road there was debris and destruction everywhere. All the houses in the street had their ceilings down, windows broken and slates off their roofs. The whole corner had disappeared! Thornhill Road corner had simply disappeared.

'In its place was a pile of rubble, although the lop-sided roofs of houses lying on piles of bricks and dust reminded you what had been there. Mr Nichols was collecting piles of tinned food from his wrecked shop-front. The laundry office girls were sorting out piles of dusty clothes. The off-licence was gone. Dr Badenoch's surgery was not there either.

'Over the way the Co-Op people were pulling out their broken windows. On the pavement trestle tables had been erected and Council officials were issuing forms to people and taking down particulars. One man nonchalantly picked up a handy half-brick from the pavement to knock a nail into place to fix a poster, then dropped it into the gutter. All the damaged shops were being tidied up by the assistants, who had reported for work as if this dreadful Sunday was a normal working day.

'We went home. Nanny burst in a few minutes later, crying and wailing. "Oh! What's happened to them all? That pretty corner! Oh! Oh!" News came from Mr Duffield over the fence at the bottom of the garden. "Mrs Ward was killed. They didn't bother to sleep in the shelter. When the bomb stopped, Mr Ward told her to put her head under the bedclothes. The lot fell on top of her. Suffocated by the time they dug her out."

'Mrs Ward was a friend of Mrs Duffield. She had a boy Jimmy and a daughter Babs. Jimmy was a little older than me. "Rotten losing your Mum," I thought. I remembered her now—a fat, jolly woman with chubby cheeks and golden hair, like Tessie O'Shea.

' "There's bombed-out all over the road. That one was *too* near," growled my father, thoughtfully.

'The door knocker sounded during lunch—corned beef, cold peas and tomatoes. It was the workmen. We had noticed swarms of them lower down the street on our walk out, carrying ladders, hammers, bags of large-headed nails, rolls of black stuff like thin lino. They nailed it over our broken windows. Mum got them some tea.

' "They've got sites all along the French coast, Belgium, Holland—wouldn't surprise me if they was in Guernsey and Jersey too," commented one elderly workman.

' "They lose six men every time they fire one," said another "Killed by the blast."

' "They say Penge has been wiped off the map," put in another.

' "Copped a bashing there then," commented Nanny.

'Kenny Salt next door called over the fence. He produced a bit of the bomb. "Found it on our chicken shed." A blackened fragment of steel with a loose bolt through it was pushed towards us. "Leave it alone!" warned Nanny. "It might go off!"

'A Mrs Adams called round. "We can get out of it. It says here in the paper. Mothers and children can be evacuated." Her husband was in the Home Guard with my Dad. Her son Derek was in my class. Always in trouble, usually with Attwood and Caudle. Some said he'd had the stick three times. I never knew his Mum knew mine.

'Dad persuaded Mum to fill up some form or other. Then a letter came. "We're all going away next Thursday," Mum announced. "We've got to report to Newport Road School." The excitement of going away, somewhere new, quite overshadowed all the buzz bombs now. I got out my atlas, turned to the England page and studied for interesting places to be evacuated to. During the 1940–41 Blitz Mum, Doug and I had spent a year at Bath. I could only dimly remember that.

'It was July now. It seemed months since we had last been to school. But it was less than 3 weeks since the first buzz bomb had fallen and Mum had declared, "You're safer home with me." Now I tried to stave off mounting excitement about going away by getting out all my jigsaw puzzles and doing them on Mum's best room carpet. They kept me occupied, specially a 1,000-piece one called "The Coronation". These puzzles were the only possessions of mine I lost due to enemy action. While we were evacuated the ceiling fell in on them and they were all swept away.

'The day before our departure Nanny came home from work complaining that she had been forced to throw herself down in the street. "One came right over and I just had to throw myself down. There was a young couple near me did the same." Earlier that afternoon we had taken our leave of the High Road in a final trip to the shops. Gangs of workmen were pulling down unsafe buildings at the top of Thornhill Road and Windsor Road. Many were in some kind of uniform, dark, swarthy men. "Italian prisoners," scoffed some passers by. One was driving a bulldozer, the first I had ever seen. He had attached a long cable to the wall of a tall building and the other end to a loop behind the driving seat. The bulldozer lunged forward. The wall above quivered. Then it fell forward, collapsing in a cloud of dust. A music shop had been on the ground floor.

'The night before we left I did not sleep a wink. Where would we be going? I was lying awake when Mum and Dad came to bed in the shelter. It was a fine evening. "Come up here and have a look," Dad called down. He gave me a hand up. We saw in the darkening sky a glimmer of red light scurrying across. "There's a buzz bomb," said Dad. I believe that one fell on the bus garage at Leyton Green.'

Sheffield was where the special evacuation train deposited them, and the twelve weeks they spent there were not altogether happy ones. Things got off to a bad start as soon as they got off the train.

'A throng of jeering onlookers lined the short walk from the train to the awaiting buses. Some weaker mothers were crying among our group. "They don't know there's a war on up 'ere," bawled a tough Leyton Mum behind us. The bus journey through the depressing, unfamiliar streets brought out more tears.'

The Kings were billeted on a lady separated from her husband with a son called Keith, 'a little horror, thoroughly spoiled by his mother'. Lionel and Douglas spent much of their time playing in the quiet street or in neighbours' gardens. Hillsborough Park became the meeting-place for Leyton families, most of them homesick.

'I suppose these meetings cheered us up. "Fed up and far from home!" the mothers used to sing as we children ran about the enormous park. They used to talk about the news from Leyton. Letters were always coming. Their contents were eagerly listened to by all. Some bombed houses had been bombed again. An Italian prisoner had been blown off the roof of a house he was demolishing . . .'

The best time was when Dad came to spend two weeks with them—the first family holiday they had had together during the war. He took them for long walks along rivers in the beautiful countryside outside Sheffield, Keith, with no father of his own, holding Dad's hand all the time. But even this happy interlude was cut short. A telegram came from Nanny: 'Come home. More trouble.' Another buzz bomb had fallen at the top of the road. The house had been badly shaken again and Nanny could not cope on her own.

One morning Mum read out a letter from Dad. 'There's a new type of bomb. Just a flash and a loud explosion. No warning it's coming.' Despite this they all wanted to go home. Mrs H., Keith's mother, became quite pleasant again when Mum announced their decision. She had begun to find fault and accuse the boys of minor damage to the house.

The day after returning to Leyton, they were back at school, a depleted school to which other evacuees trickled back as the term progressed. Buzz bombs were a rarity—now launched from planes or from launching sites in Holland. The new weapon was the V2, far more frightening than the V1 because you could not hear it coming (518 reached London, killing 2,724 and badly injuring 6,000).

'The fall of a rocket during school hours shattered our concentration for the rest of the morning or afternoon session. One occasion, just before noon, my attention was distracted by a flicker of light upon the wall just above my eye-level. I glanced at the window and, at that precise moment, a resounding explosion shook the whole school. By some uncanny instinct children always seemed to know when a V2 had fallen near their home. This time a boy called Lennie Miles suddenly burst into tears and was allowed to go home. An hour or so later we found that this bomb had fallen in Tyndall Road, near where he lived.

'On another occasion, when walking home down Crawley Road from school, something attracted my attention away to the north-west in the direction of the Midland Railway arches. There were a series of rings in the blue winter sky, quite unlike anything I had ever seen. Then came the explosion as another V2 registered itself.'

It was as late as March 1945 that Lionel made a last entry in his diary to his catalogue of rocket-bombs.

'Late one afternoon a forgotten sound once more resounded through our shattered streets. "Is that a buzz bomb?" enquired Mum, somewhat incredulous. "Yes," we both cried delightedly, rushing to the now unused shelter. The last V1 Leyton was ever to hear spluttered out somewhere not far away and exploded. "I thought we'd heard the last of them before we went to Sheffield," sighed my mother. We climbed out of the shelter for the last time, at the same time, no doubt, as countless other war-weary Leytonians sharing similar thoughts.'

Lionel King's story ends there, but there is a footnote which might suggest that his family, and indeed the whole neighbourhood, were a great deal luckier than they had ever thought during that Buzz Bomb Summer. One thing that had always disappointed him at the time was that gunners did not open fire on the buzz bombs. They had, in fact, done so for the first week of the V1 bombardment, when it was realised that shooting them down over populous areas served no purpose and London's AA guns were moved to the North Downs. It was ten years later, while browsing through the old diaries, that he came upon a puzzling incident, which, with its possible explanation, he recorded in the autobiography he had begun to write.

'On the afternoon before we left for Sheffield, at about 5 pm, we heard a buzz bomb approaching. We rushed down the garden to the shelter and, as we did so, I heard a series of pops rather like large corks being removed from a giant bottle. I thought for a moment that it might have been soldiers disobeying orders and firing at the approaching bomb with small arms. Then the engine cut out and the bomb exploded far away.

'At Grammar School almost ten years later, we were discussing the V1/V2 saga one day, and I mentioned the incident. A teacher, who had been involved in Civil Defence, recounted how on one occasion soldiers had been forced to fire at a bomb which looked as if it was heading for an arms dump in Epping Forest, behind Hollows Pond.

' "As it was beginning to fall to earth, soldiers opened up at it and deflected it," he said. "It landed, very luckily, in Hollows Pond. If it hadn't, most of Leyton would have gone up." '

10 *High Seas to Hiroshima*

'VE Day found the British Pacific Fleet at action stations east of Formosa some 600 miles south of Japan. Cloud piled high over the Sakishima islands kept our Fleet Air Arm bombers carrier-bound, while fighter sweeps failed to locate any Kamikazes. By nightfall our course was set south through driving rain and spray whipped up by wind in the howling darkness and there was leisure enough to indulge nostalgic speculations as to the celebrations at home half-way across the world. The Premier's speech was relayed throughout each ship at ten pm. Earlier the Captain of this carrier had told the 2,000 crew: "Thousands of British and American troops will now be coming out to join us. We are the vanguard." '

So I wrote in a despatch to my newspaper, the *News Chronicle*, on 8 May 1945, as a war correspondent aboard the aircraft carrier HMS *Indefatigable*, and in the wardroom that night joined the carrier's 200 officers in splicing the mainbrace. We rejoiced at the thought of the bells ringing and the lights blazing out again over England. But for us victory still seemed a long way off. No one could foresee how near Japan was to collapse. We imagined ourselves the vanguard of a huge Allied invasion force yet to be assembled. Our D-Day—let alone our V-Day—had yet to come.

For most people in Britain the war in the Pacific had always been a shadowy affair, largely the concern of the Americans. It is doubtful if many were even aware that a British Pacific Fleet had been created (by agreement between Churchill and Roosevelt) to ensure an active role for Britain in the final phases of the Far Eastern War, and that it was now engaged in a mid-ocean operation unique in naval history. With Germany defeated, the space-starved London newspapers (four pages for most dailies) were preoccupied with the aftermath of war in Europe, the return to normality on the home front, the coming general election. For the most part it was only in tucked-away paragraphs that readers were reminded that a war of mounting ferocity was still being waged the other side of the world.

It is because the closing stages of this war, as seen from the British side, have rarely been chronicled that I have felt justified in including some of my own experiences in this compilation. Up to the time I landed with American marines on the Japanese mainland, very few of the despatches, from copies of which I here quote, had been used. Even an eye-witness account of two Kamikaze attacks on the British fleet, in which nearby carriers had been struck—events that must surely have rated headlines in a European context—raised little interest. One, severely cut, was used on the back page of the *News Chronicle,* under the heading 'Jap suicide planes sent into action', next to a story headed 'Hospital ward closed: not enough nurses.'

The BPF's first engagement, as part of the American Fifth Fleet, was during Operation 'Iceberg', the invasion of Okinawa, the capture of which would at last bring Japan within range of American heavy bombers. That capture took eighty-two days, during which most of the Japanese garrison of 80,000 were wiped out at a cost of 12,000 American lives. During the first two months the British task force's unspectacular but crucial assignment was the neutralising of Japanese airfields on the group of islands known as the Sakishima Gunto, the only link between the Japanese on Formosa and the hard-pressed Okinawa garrison.

With the virtual elimination of the Japanese navy, the Allied fleet would have had an easy enough time of it had it not been for that new weapon of Japanese fanaticism, the Kamikaze. From a mass attack by some 350 suicide planes on 6 April to the end of the Okinawa campaign, it was estimated that 1,900 Kamikaze pilots took off, never to return. Most were shot down by fighters or flak before homing on a target, but 24 ships were sunk and another 202 damaged. The Kamikaze was a threat taken very seriously at the time by Allied commanders. And, even accepting that censorship played down the threat and that the British fleet itself came through relatively unscathed, it still seems remarkable that the British press showed little awareness of the menace of what can now be regarded as a manned forerunner of the deadly guided missile.

During the operation the British task force, under Vice-Admiral Sir Bernard Rawlings, comprised the battleships *King George V* and *Howe*, the aircraft carriers *Indefatigable, Illustrious, Indomitable* and *Victorious* (carrying a total of 65 bombers and 151 fighters), 5 cruisers and 11 destroyers. On the day of the first Okinawa landings, the *Indefatigable* had been hit by a suicide bomber, but had suffered minimal damage thanks to the armour-plating of her flight deck (a factor that was to save other carriers from serious harm). It was half-way through the operation that I joined her, together with John Ridley of the *Daily Telegraph*, after a four weeks' flight between the two wars, from England via Australia to the naval base at Leyte in the Philippines. Unproductive of much hard news though our accreditation was to prove, we were taking part in history of a kind. This was the longest naval operation ever undertaken, and the first time a British naval force had been kept refuelled and replenished in mid-ocean by a fleet train, a conveyor belt of tankers and supply ships operating from Leyte. What we were also witnessing was the end of an era. Never again would Britannia rule the waves in such strength, even though it was now in the shadow of a mightier American fleet.

In what follows I have interspersed extracts from despatches with extracts from letters writen to my wife-to-be in England to suggest something of what life on the ocean wave felt like to a civilian landlubber (though disguised in uniform). During the previous winter I had been attached to the American 9th and 1st armies throughout the German offensive in the Ardennes. There could have been no greater contrast between those alarms and excursions in the freezing cold of the Battle of the Bulge and the tradition-bound, orderly, almost cossetted life that now lapped us round in the sweltering below-decks heat of a great warship.

23 April. Extract from letter. 'We reached journey's end in the early morning light of Saturday when the sloop that had brought us from the Philippines came alongside this gigantic aircraft carrier in a stormy Pacific not more than 200 miles off Formosa. Here at last was the Fleet, a noble sight ploughing the leaping waves. As well as ourselves the sloop brought bags and bags of mail and the Chief of Staff—who gave us a very good briefing on the Far Eastern War during the two-day trip.

'The carrier's decks were lined with faces—interested more probably in the mail than us, although our method of transference might have intrigued them. Ropes on pulleys were strung between the two ships, which were sailing at about ten knots. We sat in a kind of chair and sailed through the air with not the greatest of ease. Those leaping waves beneath . . .

'The Fleet had completed its first operation, so we're having a lazy time in comparative luxury. My cabin is next to the Admiral's palatial quarters (actually there's no Admiral on board), roomy, well furnished, but unfortunately without a porthole. Despite fans and air vents it's very hot. I write stripped to the waist and clammy with sweat—we live in a perpetual Turkish bath. To think so recently I was knee-deep in Ardennes snow!

'The Ward Room is large and crowded with officers, a very friendly lot. Most of the Fleet Air Arm pilots are very young—a 20th birthday yesterday!—gay, sentimental, naive in some respects, ancient in others. Supplies plentiful—food, tobacco, drinks (though rationed). Only five weeks from England makes us unique. Everyone wants to know what London is like now, what about U-boats, were the trees beginning to bud. No papers, no BBC—mail is the only link with home. On the sloop John and I were inveigled into speaking on the ship's wireless—he on home news, I on Europe—to the crew of some 250. Here there are nearly 2,000 and the Commander threatens us with another talk—a more alarming prospect! So far I haven't written a thing —must do so tomorrow, though it will be very much a "think-piece" . . .

'Before leaving Sydney we were taken for a few words with Admiral Sir Bruce Fraser, the Big Chief. He hummed and heaved and paced up and down by his desk. Afterwards the PRO said: "You might think he's rather reticent and aloof, actually he's thinking ALL THE TIME"!'

4 May. Despatch (partially used on page 3, marked 'delayed' on VE Day), 'The big guns of the British Pacific Fleet today joined in the pounding of the vital Japanese airfields on the Sakashima Gunto. Fleet Air Arm bombers striking shortly after dawn had opened the second phase of the Fleet's operations in Pacific waters. Returning to their targets of two weeks ago they straddled airfield runways at Myako and Ishigaki with their 500-pounders, while rocket-firing Fireflies attacked coastal targets and flak positions.

'The bombardment was carried out by a force of battleships and cruisers. Some sixteen miles from the target fourteen-inch guns sent the crushing weight of broadsides to batter runways and perimeter. Two Corsairs spotting for the cruiser force observed excellent results. The first salvo ripped up the runway with deadly accuracy.

'While the bombardment was in progress, the aircraft carrier force, separated from the escorting battleships and cruisers, were subjected to a vicious attack by Japanese Kamikazes. The attack lasted over half an hour and was carried out by two waves of "death and glory" Zekes. From the Admiral's bridge of this carrier the scene was spectacular and confused. The attack had stirred up a hornet's nest and flights of Seafires, Hellcats and Corsairs climbed and circled in search of a kill. Meanwhile the guns of carriers and destroyers thundered and flashed until the sky was smudged with the black shell-bursts.

'Only three of the suicide pilots succeeded in penetrating the fighter screen and the curtain of flak. One rocketed down at great speed and a cloud of smoke and flame burst from one of our carriers as it struck. Black smoke poured for some minutes from the damaged ship, and through it could be seen the angry red flashes of her guns firing at another attacker. This Zeke came down in its death dive on to another carrier, hit the flight deck without exploding and bounced into the sea.

'Shortly afterwards it was followed by another. Not more than half a mile away I could see it headed in an almost vertical dive for the same carrier. There was a red flash as it was hit and a shower of smoke and spray as it dived into the sea just alongside. The speed at which it was travelling must have taken it well under for I could see no debris, no trace of it on the surface of the sea. Fire was soon extinguished in the damaged carrier, where there were some casualties. Fourteen enemy aircraft are reported shot down.'

9 May. Extract from despatch (partially used, back page, on 22 May). 'Out of a clear evening sky Japanese Kamikazes swooped for the second time in five days on heavy units of the British Pacific Fleet . . . The first two to penetrate the fighter and flak screen made for the same ship, an aircraft carrier. Both hit the flight deck and both by some lucky chance plunged from there into the sea, blazing wrecks. A Kamikaze attack is unlike anything one has known in the Western war. At the back of one's mind continually is the thought of the pilots, fanatical, cold-blooded, whose last ambition is that death might also be glory. They wear, we are told, some kind of ceremonial uniform.

'Of the death dive of a third Kamikaze I had a breath-taking view from the Admiral's bridge. Its approach was signalled as usual by the gun flashes of battleship, carrier, cruiser, destroyer, and the growing rash of smoke puffs against the clear sky. The Zeke was flying low and we could see it now speeding on level course across the Fleet, ringed round, pursued, by the bursting shells. It seemed to bear a charmed life, cutting unscathed through the murderous hail of flak. Less than a mile from us we saw it turn aft of another carrier. It was approaching its kill. The air all around was smudged and clamorous with the bursting shells, joined now by the sharper points of pom-poms firing from the carrier's decks.

'The Jap climbed suddenly and dived. It was all a matter of seconds. He came up the centre of the flight deck, accurate as a homing plane, and abruptly all was lost in a confusion of smoke and flame. The whole superstructure of the ship vanished behind billows of jet black smoke shot through by flames as the tanks of aircraft ranged on the deck exploded.

'It seemed at the time that the ship was doomed, that nothing could survive that inferno. But within half an hour the flames were extinguished and the smoke had drifted and dispersed in the sunlight. Through glasses we could see the armour plated deck of the carrier swarming with activity. The island was blackened and a hole gaped at its base, but the damage seemed negligible for all that chaos of smoke and flame. When a few weeks ago this carrier was hit by a Kamikaze, planes were taking off again within seven minutes.'

16 May. Extract from letter. 'The Norfolk holiday sounds quite delectable. Drenched in sweat in the wardroom we sometimes indulge nostalgic dreams of misty meadows at dawn, London streets in the rain, wind on the heath. Now we are nostalge-ing about Victory Day—how many times since 1939 we'd decided just what to do at the Armistice and look where we find ourselves etc. It seems ages since I was in London. I wonder has it changed much. Do lights blaze, naked and unashamed, from every window? Is some of the weariness gone? We're all terribly eager to hear about Victory Day—papers out here take two months to arrive. Are you likely soon to be released, for I see they talk of conscription up to the end of the Jap war—most people here give it about 18 months . . ."

17 May. Extract from incomplete copy of despatch (unused). 'Having many times watched the pilots and crews of Fleet Air Arm Avengers taking off and returning from the deck of this aircraft carrier, I was granted permission today to accompany them on a strike. Targets were runways and the town of Hirara on Miyako Jima, most easterly of the Sakishima group. For the layman there is some excitement in the actual takeoff and landing on an aircraft carrier. After months of trial and error the Fleet Air Arm has brought this to a fine art, though not so fine as to preclude occasional barrier crashes and other mishaps. Two of the eight Avengers in our formation today were unable to take off, their wings refusing to unfold. They retired to the side of the ship and soon we took our place and roared along the deck to dip slightly over the bows and climb.

'The leader, with undercarriage down, circled until the formation was complete and we set course for the islands. We were joined by eight Avengers from another carrier. Heat haze shrouded the horizons and patchy cloud stained the sea with shadow. It was not an ideal day for observation. Miyako, when it came into view on the starboard bow, was capped all its length by dense white cloud rising out of the haze like a snowclad mountain range.

'We rounded the cloud pack and the island, fifteen miles across at the widest point, lay beneath it, flat and arid, dead-looking and deserted. Creeks and bays were empty of shipping, roads of transport. Long since the Japanese have found cunning concealment for their aircraft in fields or caves or even amongst the tight huddle of houses. Flak if encountered at all is for the most part light and inaccurate. You would not guess that, like the other islands, is is crowded with Japanese troops and civilians.

'Approaching land, the formation had split up for their

different targets, ours the 1,200 yards long runway of Nobara airfield . . .'

30 May. Start of long despatch (*unused*). 'An operation unique in the history of the Royal Navy has just been completed. Now that we are speeding south through the blue wastes of the Pacific, south for the equator and beyond, it is timely to record the considerable achievements of this most powerful of British task forces. They have not made headline news and indeed have been covered by a few curt lines in the daily communiques. This first mission of the British Pacific Fleet was quite simply to prevent Japanese aircraft from Formosa coming to the aid of the land forces on Okinawa. To some it might have seemed a trivial assignment for so powerful a fleet—rather like cracking a walnut with a steam roller. But the High Command did not think so—and neither did the Japs . . .'

31 May. Extract from letter. 'I sometimes wish I was with an army again—plenty to do and write about and the feeling of being in the thick of things and up against realities, trenches rather than horizons . . . We're sailing now towards near-winter (52 degrees at Sydney) and no longer suffer the discomforts of perspiration. Round the equator it's nearly always raining or about to rain, but without tempering the heat in the slightest—the rain merely confirms the existing dampness of body and clothes.

'Most of the men have not seen land, except for glimpses of fetid tropical islands, for more than three months—and it's six weeks since I felt terra firma. Sea, sea and more sea, the same routine, the same company, the same walk down the oily steel corridors from cabin to wardroom—so much the same of everything that I feel by now rather like a sleep-walker. People become easily bored, peevish, or in naval vernacular "chokkah", and find an outlet in nostalgic reminiscence or anticipation, and some in bouts of strident drunkenness—the latter though is difficult as we are allowed only so much a month.

'There's not much to say about sea. And the Pacific for us

has not been the vast and terrifying enormity that a man in a sailing ship or an open boat might describe. The ships of His Majesty's Navy reassuringly punctuate the horizon and all between the waves are cut by long and glittering wakes: it has been a Pacific very much presided over by man. Only rarely has the sense of loneliness and awe overtaken me—at sunset when we recline on the quarter deck, perhaps after a gramophone recital of Beethoven or Brahms, and in moonlight on the flight deck.

'There were sunsets north of the equator such as you have never seen—all the colours of earth ebbing and flowering in the west, clouds in the east sombre purple, pale pink, and the sea shot with colour. This was something celestial and (to clinch the fancy) you might imagine as the sun dipped into the sea and a golden radiance lit the quarter deck that the bronzed and semi-naked officers were Greek gods and heroes on their couches. A full moon came out of the sea one night as round and red as a December sun, growing smaller and paler as it climbed until the ship was silver on a silver sea. The flight deck was like a seaside promenade after dinner with officers and men parading up and down its length in animated groups . . .'

The BPF, which had sailed more than 25,000 miles during its three months at sea, spent most of June at Sydney being refitted and replenished. Three weeks later it was in action again, this time as a fourth Task Group to the American Third Fleet, and this time with the Japanese mainland as its target.

With preparations for the invasion now well under way, few were aware how close Japan already was to collapse, largely owing to the ever-tightening blockade and the devastating American air raids now being launched from Okinawa. Fewer still were aware of the terrible new weapon that had emerged from the discovery of nuclear fission. On 11 July the *News Chronicle*'s 'Military Critic', whose periodical prognostications on the Far Eastern War were given more prominence than most reports of actual happenings, wrote that 'nothing has happened to alter my view that fighting may continue in and around Japan for upwards of two years". Two weeks before the first atom bomb was dropped on Hiroshima on 6 August he was ruling out August and September as likely invasion months because they constituted the 'peak of the typhoon season'.

But now at last the BPF had sailed into the limelight. It must have come as something of a surprise to readers scarcely aware of its existence to find splashed over the front pages of newspapers on 17 July the news that *King George V* had been pouring broadsides into the Nippon homeland while Fleet Air Arm bombers and fighters swarmed overhead. But for the thirteen war correspondents now attached to the Fleet the irony was that very little of the news now being splashed excitedly around came from them. Owing to the strictly limited times during which transmission of press material was allowed, our despatches were confined to 200 words and there was no guarantee that even these would reach London the same day. Most of the material used comprised agency reports from Pacific Fleet headquarters at Guam.

Of all this belated recognition of a British presence in the Pacific we were quite unaware at the time. By the time the fleet was back at action stations we had already settled back into the comfortable, enervating, inward-looking routine aboard our respective ships. I had rejoined the fleet—and a new ship, the cruiser flagship *Newfoundland*—at its intermediary base at Manus on the equator, where it was refuelling before setting off on what was to prove its last mission of the war.

12 July. Extract from letter. 'Hoping this finds you as it leaves me: which is not likely because I write in the Captain's Day Cabin of one of His Majesty's cruisers, semi-naked. Yes, I'm back again in the Pacific wilderness with the steel walls of my state apartment vibrating to machinery and whirring fans merely stirring up the hot air. Life is more intimate and more comfortable here than on the *Indefatigable* and being the only correspondent aboard I have no competition for attention—a kind of ship's giant panda, says the Padre. After we sailed from our equatorial base the Captain moved to his tiny Sea Cabin on the bridge, bequeathing me this luxury suite—sitting room, bedroom, bathroom and a very attentive steward. This very spacious desk is decorated with a utility row of books: the Navy List, King's Regulations, a Dictionary and Holy Bible: above it a very large map of the Pacific and Far East.

'There are some sixty officers aboard this ship, a very congenial lot. My first night in the ward room a number grouped around the piano while a sub-lt with a very fine baritone sang Handel arias, Schubert, Wagner: the wilder element of the Fleet Air Arm would never have tolerated such highbrowism. Two very good types are the Doc and the Bish (MO and Padre to landlubbers). Apart from writing one or two things for the ship's magazine I've been pretty idle this last week. Life on the ocean wave, as I've almost certainly stated repeatedly, lulls one to a state of passivity in which the clock only assumes significance around meal times: for example it's quite absurd to inform me that we've been at sea for a week already.

'No land for all these hundreds of miles, from the Equator to the Tropic of Cancer and on. The weather grows finer and slightly less humid. Round the Equator rain was never far away: on the deck or the bridge one could see a squall rapidly approaching like a pillar of cloud—a sudden wind out of nowhere, rain lashing down and the vast Pacific reduced to a close circle of mist and rain. Almost as suddenly it would pass on, blue sky appear and the blazing sun lap up the pools on the deck. These natural phenomena are sufficient to keep the imagination from stagnation (though books, of course, help): sunset, sunrise (our day of sailing I had to evacuate the Captain's Sea Cabin at 6 am), stars at night and the weird dazzle of phosphorescence in the ship's wake, summer lightning . . .

'I had a cable from the editor last week: "Quite rightly you have sent little during election stop this advise you we hoping for full and regular stories and features after election". This after more than a month's silence. The election of course had nothing to do with it—I'm grateful to him for suggesting an alibi!'

17 July. Despatch, as transmitted (incorporated with agency reports). 'POWERFUL UNITS OF BRITISH PACIFIC FLEET TODAY JOINED OFFENSIVE AGAINST JAP MAINLAND STOP BRITISH TASK FORCE GROUP UNDER VICEADMIRAL RAWLINGS JOINED UP WITH ADMIRAL HALSEYS THIRD FLEET STOP BEFORE DAWN TODAY BIGGEST COMBINED FLEET OF WAR SWUNG INTO ACTION STOP WHILE AMERICAN PLANES CONTINUED POUNDING OF NUMEROUS AIRFIELDS OF TOKYO PLAIN FLEET AIR ARM AVENGERS FIREFLIES CORSAIRS ROARED IN FROM SEA OVER FLAT RICE FIELDS EAST OF SENDAI LARGEST CITY OF NORTH HONSHU TO ATTACK VITAL AIRFIELDS AND INSTALLATIONS STOP SENDAI POPULATION TWO HUNDRED TWENTY THOUSAND IS GOVERNMENT CENTRE ONE HUNDRED NINETY MILES NORTH OF TOKYO STOP MEANWHILE SEAFIRES HELLCATS RANGED BLEAK WINTRY SKIES ON LOOKOUT JAP SUICIDERS STOP SO FAR NONE MATERIALISED STOP GREAT FLEET COMPRISING MORE THAN ONE HUNDRED TWENTY WARSHIPS DEPLOYED LESS THAN TWO HUNDRED MILES OFF JAP COASTLINE STOP BRITISH TASK GROUP HAD STEAMED THOUSANDS OF MILES EXSYDNEY WHERE RETIRED AFTER SAKISHIMA OPERATION STOP AS CROW FLIES WE NOW A FEW MILES NEARER LONDON THAN SYDNEY STOP JAPS UNDOUBTEDLY WISH US CROWS END.'

20 July. Start of feature despatch, transmitted when strictures relaxed during a refuelling period (unused). 'For the majority of the thousands of officers and men of the British Task Force the first days of the assault on Japan have been as uneventful as an exercise in home waters. It has required a large effort of imagination to realise that over the horizon, sometimes less than 120 miles away, lies the densely populated plain of Tokyo. Further north we have sailed to within 80 miles of the mainland. The routine of life aboard ship persists unchanged. There is no sense at all of naval history in the making.

'Absence of excitement or apprehension in this great operation is symptomatic of very low state to which Japs have been reduced.

By sea they have nothing to oppose us. There remains possibility of massed attack by suicide planes. Our fighter pilots and gunners are vigilant for such an eventuality. Seems more likely however they will conserve these weapons of fanatic desperation for final invasion of homeland. Psychological effect on Jap people of great Allied Fleet trailing coat unchallenged in home waters cannot be overestimated.

'To give true picture of what this first assault on Japan means to average naval man it essential to rule out all heroics. Except for Fleet Air Arm pilots, who alone have actual combat with enemy, this is an abstract kind of warfare, a matter of intricate machinery and precise mathematics. Our location is a pinpoint on a map, a point that looks remarkably close at times to hostile territory. But the world remains one of sea and sky, rain and sun. At times the great battleships and carriers of the American Fleet loom on the horizon. Their presence adds to feeling of security. To officers and men who have seen action in Mediterranean, Atlantic, North Sea, absence of suspense is something new . . .'

25 July. Extract from letter. 'I've just come from the quarter deck—rain, a delicious drizzle, is falling, the sea is grey and foam-flecked vanishing into a cold mist: a sight wonderfully reminiscent of the Irish Sea and yet less than forty-five minutes flying distance away civilians are walking about the streets of mythical Japan, with umbrellas probably and listening for the throb of plane engines and crack of ack-ack guns . . .

'We heard the election results on Tuesday night after returning to the ward room from seeing a film called 'Lost Angel'. No one had the slightest doubt but that the Conservatives would be returned. The news was electrifying and is still Topic No 1, indeed Tonic No 1 too for only a very small number are of opinion that "in the view of this House this is a bad day for England". Speculations as to Cabinet, immediate reforms, the fate of Churchill etc are endlessly intriguing. Prize reaction when we first heard the news was the Commander's: in his deep pompous voice he boomed, "Well I only hope they insist on red rear lights for cyclists . . ." We all agree that Ellen Wilkinson should become First Lady of the Admiralty . . .

'Today, 28th, we are at it again and wondering whether the Japs incensed by the peace offer will launch an air attack. They tried a small-scale affair on Wed but were chased away by fighters. One plane though towards sunset was shot down almost directly above us at well over 20,000 feet. Its blossoming into flame and seemingly slow spiral descent to smoky dissolution was spectacular enough—far more so was the sight of the Jap pilot whose parachute had failed to open, plunging after it through space, twisting and turning for seconds on end before hitting the sea in a shower of spray. His body was picked up. And that was the first Jap I have seen during the entire war . . .

'Ever since my first despatch was passed round the ship the Padre has never tired of asking me whether I have "pounded" the Japs today or merely "hammered" them: I have promised to "pulverise" at the earliest opportunity . . .

'Someone brought me a flying fish the other day—it had been washed on board: a lovely thing with the body of a mackerel, blue and silver, and the wings incredibly filmy and sensitive. Unfortunately it very soon began to stink powerfully and I had to throw it away—otherwise I might have enclosed a wing . . .'

Nine days after that letter was sent the atomic bomb was dropped on Hiroshima and the war that had seemed to be dragging on indefinitely was all but over. Yet the fighting went on. On 9 August, the day the second atomic bomb burst over Nagasaki, HMS *Newfoundland* and another British cruiser joined a group of American warships in the daylight bombardment of the iron works at Kamaishi, while Kamikazes in some numbers had their last fling against the Third Fleet. But I was no longer aboard the *Newfoundland*. No longer with the BPF.

21 August. Extract from letter. 'Iwo Jima. As you will doubtless have observed the fleet operations off Japan were a flop as far as we correspondents were concerned. With a 200 word maximum per story and no certainty of even that amount getting through in time it was small wonder London offices became impatient. Some correspondents returned in exasperation to Sydney. Three weeks ago I received a cable from the office "Please report to SEAC HQ earliest"—ie Ceylon and presumably for an invasion of Singapore. It was with genuine reluctance (as Fitzpatrick would say) that I bade farewell to the *Newfoundland* and boarded another cruiser, the *Black Prince,* which was retiring to Sydney.

'After a week's sailing the first news of the surrender reached us, celebrated with formal dinner and champagne. Next morning we reached Manus on the equator and I disembarked. It seemed pointless now to spend at least the next fortnight proceeding to Ceylon for a non-existent war so I decided to make my way north again to Guam. It took three days to persuade the air transport people that my journey was both urgent and necessary but to cut a long and dull story short I reached Guam two days ago after three days' Dakota-hopping among the Pacific islands.

'Guam, Admiral Nimitz's HQ, is by comparison with other bases a fabulous place. Correspondents are spoon-fed with news, living quarters are near perfect: there is a huge open-air cinema like a Roman amphitheatre, an officers' club with a terrace overlooking a magnificent sweep of the harbour and green hills. Most of the correspondents had already left for the invasion of Japan, still pending, and yesterday I followed on their heels, a four-hour flight to this miserable war-battered island. Now I'm aboard an American ship shortly sailing to catch up the Third Fleet. What I shall see and whether I shall be allowed to go ashore is still in the lap of the gods. I devoutly hope there will be big enough news to convince the office that my decision was a right one—there being no time to ask their approval. It's depressing to think how much work and worry it has required to make a full circle from the fleet and back again! . . .

'We are now about two and a half days out from Iwo and

last night joined up with a sizeable convoy. It's getting cooler though flying fish still skim the wavetops and fans whirr inside all the time. Perhaps I shall be able to send you a postcard from Tokyo or a piece of the Imperial Palace or a cherry blossom . . .'

28 August. Despatch (used). 'Eighty miles away the peak of Fujiyama pierced the clouds early this morning. As the sun rose higher vague outlines solidified within the contours of a volcano. This was Japan.

'Seabirds wheeled and dipped about the bows of our ships. If the Japanese believed in the transmigration of the soul they might credit them with the thwarted instincts of Kamikaze pilots. Birds apart, the only activity this blue autumnal day is that of wind on water and the churning of propellers.

'Nine days out from Iwojima we had grown impatient for this sight. Now that it is before us it seems unbelievably tranquil. Crews line the ships' sides with eyes fixed on the distance, where white cloud unveils another range of mountains. Now, less than half a mile away, the island of Oshima, guarding the entrance to Sagami Bay, towers from the sea. The Japanese garrison on the cliff-tops have a ringside seat as the ships of the Allied Fleets steam past towards Tokyo.

'Three weeks ago we had imagined these shores as immeasurably hostile—the final and bloodiest goal. Only now, as we head into the shelter of the bay, watching the mainland materialise, are the implications of peace fully realised. This is an American ship, and today is a day predominantly of American triumph. It has been a long journey—not to be measured by month or mile—a journey through the valley of the shadow: thousands have not made it.

'In the past two weeks I have seen some of the places where they fell, backwaters now, where the instruments of war are typewriters and telephones and transport planes. From Manus, on the Equator, I flew for three days north, hopping among those Pacific islands whose names the years will make legendary: Leyte, Peleliu, Guam, Iwojima. The Marines who stormed their beaches and sweated through clinging jungles are remembered by the neat lines of crosses, a tiny chapel, by rusty junk that litters the coral or roofs a native hut, by the splintered trunks of palms.

'On Peleliu (with Iwojima probably the vilest of all the Pacific battlefields) the slopes of "Bloody Nose Ridge" are a chaos of blasted trees and broken rock. Nearly 1,200 Marines from one division perished on this island, and 5,000 were wounded. It is now a refuelling stop for transport planes, where passengers can drink coffee in the canteen, shaded from the burning sun.

'From the wreckage of war on Guam, a vast settlement of huts has sprung up for the American Fleet. Ratings tend flower-beds between trim concrete paths. Officers on the club terrace look down over the rim of a glass at a harbour busy with shipping. At night thousands flock to the great amphitheatre on a hill slope. Guam is a self-contained city of huts, where slovenliness of dress is a chargeable offence. But its foundations are blood.

'North across the wilderness of water four hours' flying brings us to Iwojima—dismal rubbish heap of volcanic rock and scrub. This was the "beach-head in hell", graveyard of 5,400 Marines where 16,000 wounded later died. Bulldozers have been at work on its eight square miles of sulphur-steaming rock, their blades even decapitating Mount Suribachi. Now, on their last journeys before Japan, planes land on some of the longest runways in the Pacific.

'Off-shore the American communication ship *Ancon* awaited us. Two days later we were one of a strangely assorted convoy—supply ships, submarine tenders, tugs, tankers, with four large hospital ships, one of them British, glittering with light in the darkness. The *Ancon* has come the hard way to Tokyo and her war record exemplifies the long, bitter struggle to final victory. Four years ago she was a passenger freighter plying between New York and Panama, returning with holds stacked with bananas. Since then she has taken part in all the major European landings, acting as flagship to American admirals in Morocco, Sicily, Salerno and off the Normandy beaches. In the Pacific she has participated at Saipan, Okinawa, Manila and Iwojima. And now to her falls the role of transmitting to the world the news of Japan's final surrender.'

30 August. Despatch (partially used). 'This is the diary of a war's end. The formal ceremony of surrender has yet to be enacted, but with the landing of the first waves of American and British Marines on the shores of Tokyo Bay this morning defeat has come home to the people of Japan.

'The diary starts aboard an assault craft half a mile from the shore. The time is 9 am on a serene, autumnal morning with the low tree-clad hills round the bay hazed with heat. Far to the north the massive pyramid of Fujiyama towers in mist. For the past hour we have been circling with other landing craft waiting to go in. Thirty-six fully armed Marines are crowded in the body of the boat. But the only shooting is being done by cameramen in a craft marked 'CINCPAC NEWSREEL' which has just flashed past towards the shore.

'Behind us the sea is congested with shipping—warships, transports, more and more assault craft. At the entrance to Yokosuka Harbour lies the fire-scorched hulk of the Jap battleship *Nagato*, pounded by American carrier planes during the Fleet's last operation off Japan. Her guns are still intact but the island is a mass of twisted metal. A formation of Fortresses carrying General MacArthur's airborne troops passes high overhead, a silver spear-point aimed at Tokyo. Carrier planes are weaving back and forth over the beaches. Now we have the signal to go in. The wake of the assault craft ahead of us leaps into a foam of spray.

'10 am. Half an hour ago the second wave of assault craft hit the beach. Through a few feet of water we scrambled to a seaplane ramp. On the concrete waterfront movie cameras were already whirring. An air of fantasy infuses the proceedings as uniformed Jap gendarmes and civil police stare open-mouthed but impassive at Marines marching, Marines splashing ashore, Marines searching the cavernous hangars, Marines merely staring back at the inscrutable enemy. We are ahead of schedule and the official surrender has yet to take place. But the Stars and Stripes has been unfurled on the waterfront and floats above the wreckage of a hangar.

'A Jap interpreter speaking perfect English in a near whisper is surrounded by correspondents. Hajime Onisis, naval Warrant Officer (Retired) is ready with all the answers. How have the people reacted to defeat? "We have been at war for twelve years. The people are relieved. There will be no disturbances, the people are very quiet. But the food situation is acute. The average civilian diet is sweet potatoes and rice but even the latter is short. The troops have done better but even with us meat has been very scarce." How many times has Yokosuka been bombed? He flashes a smile: "Too many times".

'Japanese cars and trucks are lined up on the waterfront for our use. The only civilians so far in evidence are neatly dressed professors of English from Jap schools and colleges. They are distinguished by white arm bands and are all teeth and affability as they offer their services as interpreters. One of them studied philosophy at America's Columbia University. With a smile he adds "I lost all my money at Coney Island when I was twenty." The English-speaking Japs are ringed by curious Marines. The Japs fluctuate between affability and timidity.

'11 am. Ceremoniously the American flag is rung up on the flagpole facing a camouflaged barrack block—the camouflage takes the form of a map of Japan and America, with distances indicated. The Brigade Colonel and a detachment of Marines stand to attention, salute and disperse. Groups of Yanks not posted for special duties are wandering about rather aimlessly, examining the neat stacks of small arms and ammunition displayed and labelled in one of the hangars like exhibits at a bazaar. Other side shows are the assortment of fighters and bombers in this hangar, where correspondents perched on boxes and fire extinguishers pound away at typewriters. The first tank, the first jeep and the first dog—a cocker spaniel—have now come ashore. To date there has been no confetti.

'Noon. From the battered bridge of the *Nagato,* 33,000 ton battleship, last hope of the Jap Navy, Tokyo Bay seems to be full of Allied shipping. The *Nagato* was boarded at eight this morning by a prize crew from the American battleship *South Dakota.* The Japs had done a thorough job of stripping the shattered battlewagon. There is little left but junk, including a pile of mattresses which might have been for purposes of harikari. Only a dozen Jap officers remained aboard. From the depths of the gloomy ship came the sound of Jap gramophone music.

'1 pm. South of the Naval Air Station we make our second landing at the naval base proper. Signs of occupation are now numerous: the first bulldozers are at work. It was here that the Japanese press were waiting to meet the Marines as they scrambled ashore. One Tokyo correspondent in his eagerness to get in the first news of the occupation had brought a basketful of carrier pigeons. In the Naval Base where I write there is some confusion in a corner where two Jap reporters are alternately interviewing and being interviewed by American correspondents. They tell us that reports of mass suicides in front of the Imperial Palace have been greatly exaggerated: only a dozen or so, including the President of the Patriotic Society, have chosen harikari. To reach this HQ we drove through tree-lined suburbs and a deserted shopping district. No civilians apart from those on special duties are being allowed in the zone of occupation. Allied troops have been warned that looting or souvenir hunting will be very severely dealt with.

'2 pm. Everything has gone according to plan and all the American and British troops are in full occupation of their respective districts. Heavy gear is now being unloaded, including water purification plants and bulldozers. Admiral Nimitz and Admiral Halsey will tour the base this afternoon. They are already ashore.'

After all those timeless weeks at sea with little to report it was now a hectic rush to see what there was to see and file copy in time for an edition. There were the first impressions of Tokyo —vast areas of it obliterated by fire bombs and high explosive, where tens of thousands of half-starving families now lived in makeshift hovels: atrocity stories by released prisoners: the bizarre pageantry aboard the US battleship *Missouri* in Tokyo Bay on 2 September, with General MacArthur, Supreme Allied Commander, acting god amongst the bemedalled top brass of nine nations as Mamoru Shigemitsu, the bespectacled Japanese Foreign Minister, in frock coat and silk top-hat, came aboard to sign the official document of surrender, the silence as he crossed the deck under the gaze of over 300 Allied correspondents only broken by the whirr of cinecameras and the clump of his peg leg.

But the most significant story of the war lay 500 miles from Tokyo. On the morning of 3 September, David Divine, correspondent with Kemsley Newspapers, and I walked past the ticket collector at Tokyo Central Station and boarded the jam-packed train for Hiroshima. Back in Tokyo three days later I filed what should have been my biggest story of the war. I was never able to discover how all but two slips of it went astray in transmission "via Navy Radio to San Francisco and Western Union to News Chronicle London". In its place the paper splashed on page one what I described in a letter to my wife-to-be as "a feature that may have been too light for NC taste". It was about the forty-two hours we had spent in the crowded trains to and from Hiroshima, and was headlined "The First Journey Through Unoccupied Japan".

My copy of the Hiroshima despatch has since been lost, and what follows is a brief piece based on it I wrote shortly after the war for the *Inky Way Annual,* followed by an extract from the feature article.

'The train was quite the most crowded I have seen. Passengers oozed from its windows and doors. It steamed and stank.

'My companion, David Divine of Kemsley, knew as much of

the language as I: not a word. It would be difficult as well as inadvisable to bluff our way to seats. Our presence at Tokyo Central four days after the Marines' landing had already aroused a certain amount of inscrutable attention.

'We sought the guard. And luck threw in our path two Frenchmen, ex-internees Kobe-bound. They had appropriated a compartment designed for train attendants in the days when there were any. Four feet by ten—but comparative breathing-space.

'The Frenchmen provided not only companionship but tins of tunny fish, smoked oysters and Japanese sauerkraut. Our own provisions for the 20-hour 500-mile journey were one K ration, a large tin of peaches and two sticks of chewing gum—all we had been able to scrounge after our snap-decision the night before.

'There had been rumours that Peter Burchett of the *Daily Express* had plunged into the blue before us and that a party of American correspondents were making the trip by air. We were spared the knowledge that this was in fact so as we sweated the day through in our cubicle, counting the hours to Hiroshima.

'In the dark before dawn we alighted on that roofless station. At the entrance we backed from a group of Japs huddled among their bundles of salvage. Beyond, night hid what we had come to see.

'A group of railway workers drowsed on benches round a brazier-fire. No one spoke as we joined them. Their masked indifference was far more disturbing than the toothy obsequities of the guard.

'But light filtered at last and we made for the open. The sun shimmered on blue distant hills . . . the curtain rose.

'We were walking on tram-lines. Ahead and on either side was —nothing. Nothing but bats flitting above tangled wires, spirals of smoke from pulverised debris. Then light touched the solitary finger of a chimney pointing at the sky . . . the bulk of a crumpled building . . . a cluster of burnt-out trams.

' "Punctuation-marks on a blank sheet . . ."—the slick phrases began to form. They would be quite inadequate to the scene as it unfolded in the radiance of this autumnal dawn. It was in signs of life that the horror was glimpsed: the cry of a baby from a factory-ruin: the old man under the broken church stairway coaxing flame from a heap of twigs, blind to our intrusion: the ashes laid out on tiles marked with paper-scrawls like bazaar exhibits: the couple emerging from underground, noses and mouths protected by muslin pads from the stench—or the presence—of death: the soldier singing lustily, as though all was right with the world, from a tent encampment.

'For two hours we walked, noting strange and terrible effects of blast and heat. There were more people about than I had anticipated, but for all their concern we might have been ghosts. We made no contact until we found a hospital, relatively habitable. Its floors were littered with wounded, the worst cases protected from flies under netted frames. Officials received us with oriental courtesy and little English. Our phonetic phrase-book ("Can you direct me to the pleasure-gardens?") did not answer the purpose.

'At length a nurse-interpreter materialised. Over a breakfast of biscuits and condensed milk we attempted to build up some picture of that fateful morning a month ago.

'Impossible. Doctor and matron answered politely, patiently, precisely. The Bomb might have been an Act of God, regrettable but inevitable: difficult to describe. The Doctor had been fortunate: only six fractures . . . I had to look again through the shattered windows to the place where thousands of the dead who still required it had been cremated to jerk their story into perspective.

'An Army truck was procured to drive us to the Praefecture some miles out. We might have been expected, honoured guests: such bowing and baring of teeth, pidgin English and gesticulations: and a meal of hash and beans. I was almost relieved amid it all to observe bitter hostility in the glance of one police officer who did not move from his desk. Before him lay a small casket. We were later informed, apologetically, that it contained the ashes of his parents, that he was upset.'

'In the blaze of evening we stood again on the roofless station. There, at the eleventh hour, to be challenged. A gendarme officer walked briskly up to us, clicked his heels, and, through the medium of a girl who spoke fluent Hollywood English, snapped out a fusillade of questions.

'Who were we? By what authority were we here? What was our business? Our names? Our rank? Our destination?

'At the curt voice of Authority a crowd of bystanders had encircled us. They craned, silently, no evasion now in their hard hostile stare. But the officer seemed satisfied with our replies—we said we had the authority of General MacArthur—clicked his heels again and strode away. Reluctantly, with glowering backward glances, the crowd dispersed.

'On the return trip we were forced to join the battle of the aisles: in exclusively Japanese company it seemed inadvisable to play an aggressive role at the outset. It was not for five hours, at a halt, that we were able to infiltrate two vacated seats.

'On this journey we had over-much leisure to observe the Nipponese character in defeat. Although travelling through areas where no non-neutral white man had trod since the beginning of the war, we were treated to a studied indifference. The only exception was a child in arms who at first sight of the inscrutable face of the Occident hid behind her mother and soon diverted her attentions to a hideous old baboon in the corner seat.

'Two tough-looking Army men, in whose features one could read the potentialities of the beast, were absorbed for half an hour in playing with the child's toy dog, zipping the fastener in its back, wagging its head, tweaking its nose, with expressions of absorbed delight. It required no little imagination to transform some of the more likely-looking of our train companions into the yellow men of the jungles, the callous torturers and fanatic fighters. It was not beyond reason, however, that the set mask that could relax into childish delight could also harden into brutality.

'Poverty and deprivation were implicit in this compartment of the Tokyo express. The men's uniforms (even civilian attire has the appearance of uniform) were coarse and shabby: the women's baggy trousers, which by Government order have replaced the kimono, clean but worn. The child in arms was fed on powdered milk and water, the former administered like distemper powder to a dog. Adult chopsticks shovelled in quantities of insipid rice with wolfish appetite. Cheaply aromatic cigarettes were smoked in stages, each puff a luxury ration.

'To turn from these alien faces and the smoky, soot-infested compartment to the countryside through which we sped was to step into the Shangri-La of fiction. In the country of the interior, green and lovely beyond all expectation, and the blue-misted mountains circling the Inland Sea, the exquisite undertones of Oriental poetry came to shimmering life.

'The barren wastes of the semi-obliterated cities we had seen —Tokyo, Yokohama, Osaka, Nagoya, Kobe—man-made wildernesses of rusted tin, pulverised masonry, charred wood, provided the violent contrast between the old and the new Japan. Every yard of available soil was under cultivation: apart from the remote mountains and the forests and copses of fir, pine, willow, bamboo, the Japanese countryside is like a universal kitchen garden.

'Men and women, bare-footed, with large sunhats and bright attire, worked industriously in the acres of cool rice and millet and on the terraced tea plantations. Thatched farms, self-contained behind high-clipped hedges, and trim villages with high gables and fluted tiles showing through the trees, have escaped the "enlightenments" of modern civilisation. Shinto and Buddhist shrines and temples adorn the leafy hillsides. Was it for weariness of this inheritance that the Japs fought like tigers for possession of the barren islands of the Pacific, the jungles of Burma?

'Ambition is without reason, but one cannot resist the thought that feudal Japan of a hundred years ago was a happy state compared to the ravaged country of today. Westernised civilisation opened Japan to the tourist—and to the conqueror. Thanks to it one can sit in a Tokyo express running amazingly to schedule and view the relics of cities and the sufferings of a nation. Out of the ruins and the twisted minds there is still the chance of a return to sanity. In place of the rifle the Jap soldier holds a child's toy and the smile that replaces the brute grimace may be more than an illusion of peaceable disposition.'

Notes on Contributors

Where certain biographical details are contained in a chapter, they are not repeated in these notes.

1 Dunkirk Driver

W. B. A. Gaze spent the last four years of the war in the Far East, mostly as Sergeant Acting Quarter-master in the RIEME. He took part in the Burma campaign in 1944 with the 20th Indian Division and finished the war at Saigon, his last assignment being instructor to the Foreign Legion. Today he is still an active partner with his two sons in four farms in Norfolk and Suffolk.

In 1972 Gaze made his first return visit to Dunkirk and found almost everything changed. 'Only the Chateau Rosendale, now an orphanage, was almost exactly as I remembered it, though the grounds have been made into a little park, with an ornamental lake in place of the dirty pond from which I brought water to the wounded. But I found the place where we buried 140 men in a strawberry bed. It is still known as the *cimetière* and I was able to point out to the orphanage *directeur* where I had buried many arms and legs—not to mention rifles.'

2 Retreat from Abbeville

John Steachen Brown, who died in 1961, was born at Goole, East Yorkshire, in 1904, son of a master slater. He married in 1931 and had one son, He joined the Territorials early in 1939 and was called up with the KOYLI in August. When admitted to Leeds

Hospital after the ordeal described in his diary, gangrene was feared and a toenail removed. After sick leave he rejoined his company and was sent to an OCTU. For the rest of the war he served as an officer with the 33rd Indian Corps in Burma. He returned to his work as Managing Clerk with a Wakefield firm of solicitors where he remained until his death.

The diary was found by a secondhand bookseller and sent to the Imperial War Museum. 'It got to the bookseller's by mistake,' writes his widow. 'My husband was a book-worm and had a large collection of books which I sold after his death. I have no idea how the diary came to be amongst them—he had always kept it in a file with his service papers. To the best of my knowledge no one had ever read it but myself. He rarely talked about his war experiences. He was by no means the popular conception of a blunt Yorkshireman, being quietly spoken, well mannered.'

3 Battle Honour in Tunisia

John Clark, who describes himself as 'very much of East Midlands stock, with both my parents' families active in the Methodist Movement', was educated at local council school and Scunthorpe Grammar School before going to Oxford. After his capture by the Germans he spent two years in prison camps in Italy and Germany, and narrowly escaped death shortly before his liberation by 3rd Army troops on 29 April 1945. The column of POWs in which he was being marched south in Bavaria was fired on by American fighters: eleven were killed, forty-two wounded.

Clark is now a careers master at a school in Bedford. He married, in 1954, a girl he had known as a schoolboy, and has two daughters.

Of the scenes in his account that he has put into a loose verse form he writes: 'I have tried to write an objective account of these scenes but I can't—my feelings won't "uncompress".'

4 The Cook's Tale

Ted Smith has no relics left of his years in the army except a tattered pay book, his medical discharge papers and some faded snapshots of himself posing in swimming trunks on Tunisian beaches with the French families he befriended. 'I twice lost all my gear, once on going into hospital in Tunis, then at Weymouth," he writes. 'All my German badges, buckles, swastikas, the lot, all gone, and I've only seen two or three of that crowd in all that time since. It's sometimes hard to imagine that this war ever happened, it all seems like a dream.'

5 Stalag III D—Berlin

Norman Norris came from a working-class family at Peckham. His father, who served in the Machine Gun Corps in World War I, was also taken prisoner and endured an even grimmer ordeal than his son was to experience, being made to work in the iron ore mines at Metz. On his discharge from the army, Norris, who had worked for a tea company in the city before the war, went into engineering and is now employed by a company manufacturing industrial controls in Kingston-on-Thames, Surrey.

With reference to the Germans' use of POWs on railway construction and other work directly related to the war effort, Norris writes: 'I can only say that the loaded rifle made everything legitimate—I well remember "going on strike" with three other POWs only to find ourselves working with a rifle in our backs. Unfortunately much glamour has been written and filmed about POW life in Germany. It was a totally different world for the officers living in their camps.'

6 Prisoners of the Japs

Leonard Marsh lives at Stevenage, Herts, and for the past nineteen years has held managerial positions in the Post Office. His outside interests are church work, scouting and the Rotarians. He is married with two grown-up sons.

T. E. Walter married ten months after his return to England. In 1946 he went to Southern Rhodesia as a Government Forest Officer, two years later emigrated to Ceylon as Scientific Officer with the Tea Research Institute. He returned to England in 1956 with his wife and three children to become Assistant Scientific Officer at East Malling Research Station. In 1967 he was transferred to the Commonwealth Bureau of Horticulture and Plantation Crops as a Scientific Information Officer. In work connected with horticultural literature he has found the knowledge of Dutch he acquired as a POW 'an invaluable qualification'.

7 *Love and War*
Mrs Joan Veazey, born in 1914, was educated at Sutton and Shrewsbury GPDST schools, later took courses in domestic science, children's nursing and art. She describes her childhood as 'very happy' and her parents (who lost everything during the 'Slump') as 'devoted to each other'.

Her husband was Vicar of St Silas Church, Nunhead, London SE11, from 1941 to 1957, when he became Vicar of Doddington, near Sittingbourne, Kent. She is today a professional calligraphist (having taken a course at the Slade School of Fine Art in 1956) and a breeder of blue persians. Their daughter and son are both married and they have two grand-daughters. Mrs Veazey describes her marriage as 'exceedingly happy—without a single quarrel as yet."

8 *Diary of a Somerset Housewife*
Mrs Anne Lee-Michell was born Anne Garnett at Highgate, London, in 1908. 'Garnetts apparently go on writing for ever without undue effort,' she says with reference to her war diary. Her mother wrote novels (*The Infamous John Friend* was serialised on television) and her father 'joyous short stories' for Blackwoods, later published in book form—'perfect examples of their kind, he had such a light touch'. David Garnett is a first cousin.

Mrs Lee-Michell spent much of her youth in West Somerset, where she met her husband. Since his retirement in 1962 they have lived at Milverton, Somerset, six miles from the scenes described in the diary. Their two daughters are married and there are six grandchildren. 'Babs' is as great a friend as ever, 'Beatrice' still comes to stay, the Australians have become lifelong friends, with happy reunions when they come to England. Nothing more has been heard of 'Texan Bill'. Mrs Lee-Michell wears a battle-jacket he left behind, for gardening.

9 *Buzz Bomb Summer*
Lionel King became a teacher in the West Midlands after studying at Birmingham University, and is now a lecturer in Liberal Education at West Bromwich College of Technology. He has twice been an unsuccessful candidate at parliamentary elections and lists 'poli-

tics and recent history' as his chief hobby. He is married with a son and daughter.

His brother Douglas is now in shipping insurance in the City. His Aunt Joyce married a GI in 1944, divorced and remarried in 1950. His parents still live at the old address in Leyton, his father now being employed as a senior postal clerk with a City firm. Of his grandmother, who died in 1961, King writes: 'She admitted secretly that Hitler had done a lot to clear London slums in which she had lived much of her life!'

10 High Seas to Hiroshima

Born in 1919, educated at Birkenhead School where he trained with the OTC, Michael Moynihan saw more of the last war than many of his contemporaries despite having been medically rejected for the Services. After a provincial grounding as a reporter (when he served with the Home Guard) he joined the *News Chronicle* in London in 1942 and became the youngest British war correspondent shortly before D-Day.

He was first accredited to the 2nd Tactical Air Force in Normandy, where he followed through the Falaise Gap 'massacre' to the liberation of Paris. A number of operational flights he made as an observer included the bombing of V1 rocket launching sites and the towing of gliders to Arnhem. He was attached to the American 9th and 1st Armies through the bitter winter's Battle of the Bulge in the Ardennes. During the last five months of the Far Eastern War he was accredited to the British Pacific Fleet, witnessing two Kamikaze attacks, finally landing with American Marines in Tokyo Bay and becoming one of the first correspondents to walk through the ruins of Hiroshima.

After the closure of the *News Chronicle* in 1960, Moynihan joined the *Observer,* moving to *The Sunday Times* in 1962, where he has since worked as a news and feature writer. He is married, with a son and daughter.